THE 100 GREATEST DESSERTS OF THE SOUTH

THE 100 GREATEST DESSERTS OF THE SOUTH

MARY LEIGH FURRH
AND JO BARKSDALE

Pelican Publishing Company
Gretna 2008

The word "Pelican" and the depiction of a pelican
are trademarks of Pelican Publishing Company, Inc.,
and are registered in the U.S. Patent and Trademark Office.

Library of Congress Cataloging-in-Publication Data

Furrh, Mary Leigh.
  The 100 greatest desserts of the South / Mary Leigh Furrh
and Jo Barksdale.
      p. cm.
  Includes index.
  ISBN 978-1-58980-613-9 (pbk. : alk. paper) 1.
Desserts—Southern States. 2. Cookery, American—Southern
style. I. Barksdale, Jo. II. Title. III. Title: One hundred
greatest desserts of the South.
  TX773.F85 2008
  641.8'6—dc22

                                          2008022254

Printed in the United States of America
Published by Pelican Publishing Company, Inc.
1000 Burmaster Street, Gretna, Louisiana 70053

CONTENTS

INTRODUCTION

Desserts have been popular in the South since the first settlers arrived in Virginia with visions of English puddings and double-crusted pies. By the early 1700s, the colonies were on the brink of establishing a civilized society in which the proper preparation and serving of food were important. Native fruits, nuts, dairy products, imported seasonings, and extracts were used to create desserts which were made by European rules but had a distinctly American flavor.

For many years, sugar was impractical and costly to use. It was sold in hard cones sometimes weighing ten pounds and requiring tedious chipping to produce usable crystals. It was so expensive that only the wealthy could afford it. Consequently, molasses was the usual sweetener.

Williamsburg was the first center of festive entertaining in the South. The seat of the state's government, it was the scene of numerous balls and parties when the Assembly was in session. The hosts' English heritage was obvious at these affairs, which featured lavish assortments of creams, jellies, molds, and puddings, placed side by side on a separate table from the entrees.

The French influence appeared when Thomas Jefferson returned from serving as minister to France with recipes for Charlotte Russe, meringues, and other French sweets. Virginia hostesses welcomed these pretty delicacies and added them to the spectacular displays on their dessert tables. Indeed, looks were so important to colonial cooks that they often tinted desserts with spinach or beet juice, oblivious to the strange tastes that resulted.

Further south, Charleston soon became another important center of fine cuisine. The French Huguenot influence united with the English to popularize soufflés, boiled custards, and whipped cream creations. The city's humidity prevented pie crusts from turning out well, so recipes using lady fingers came into vogue. During the slavery period and later, when servants were plentiful, it was customary in

Charleston for the lady of the house to make the dessert. This was particularly true of cake making—a time-consuming job requiring spices to be hand-ground, flour to be dried, and butter to be washed free of salt. A reputation for making good cakes was a source of pride.

Famous Charleston benne wafers owe their origins to black cooks who brought benne seeds (sesame seeds) from Africa, but the black influence is more evident in New Orleans desserts than in those of Virginia and South Carolina. Creative slaves used their talents for combining spices to flavor Creole sweets as well as other Louisiana foods.

Before the Civil War, New Orleans was a sophisticated city where luxury-loving Creoles enjoyed a fashionable social life highlighted by elaborate masked balls and stylish dinners. Planters from River Road plantations often owned town houses in the Vieux Carré, where they spent the winter attending operas and plays and revelling in the city's fast-paced social scene. Space was at a premium and houses were joined together directly on the sidewalks. Street vendors were a familiar sight on French Quarter streets, especially the pralinières who sold Pralines and the Calas women who hawked their spicy breakfast cakes on cool mornings.

The Mississippi River was the great thoroughfare of the middle South. Imported foods were shipped upstream with French furniture and Italian mantels to the mansions of the planter aristocracy along the River Road and in Natchez. Before 1830, cotton was king and Natchez boasted more millionaires than any other city in the United States except New York. Setting a fine table was a top priority with wealthy Natchezians, and elegant parties featuring sumptuous desserts took place.

In rural areas on the Mississippi, plantation life was similar to that throughout the South. A tremendous amount of cooking was necessary to feed the owners' families and slaves plus a constant flow of visitors. Distances between towns were great and inns were scarce; travelers stopped at plantations unannounced to spend the night and often lingered for weeks. The strain on household budgets could be severe: George Washington and Thomas Jefferson suffered financial difficulties brought on by the continual influx of visitors to Mount Vernon and Monticello.

Dinner was served in mid-afternoon on most plantations, and the variety and amount of food was staggering. Diners had several choices of pies, puddings, and custards, and they consumed as many servings as they pleased. In early evening, a light meal similar to English tea was presented with cookies, cakes, and tea breads. The constant cooking kept mistress and slave in the kitchen for hours.

Because plantations were self-sufficient entities, the planter's wife was usually an excellent manager, who was unlike the frivolous creature portrayed in popular novels. She found it necessary to practice strict economy and make do with food raised on the land. Her mentor was her black cook—a genius at improvisation. The women became adept at turning plantation-grown sweet potatoes, fruit, nuts, and dairy products into tasty desserts, using recipes from the few available cookbooks or creating them as they went along.

Resourcefulness was also evident in the pioneer states of Kentucky, Tennessee, and Texas. Old cookbooks reveal that pies were the most popular desserts on the frontier. They were made with whatever the hardy settlers had on hand: vinegar, jam, raisins, and fruit. Inventive cooks worked wonders with puddings, seasoning them with spices and creating sauces flavored with spirits.

The Civil War brought the South to its knees and the harsh realities of Reconstruction dismissed entertaining as a trivial concern. Even in such dire circumstances, Southerners found comfort in getting together with friends for simple parties where the only refreshments were inexpensive sweets. When prosperity finally returned, Southern hospitality was evident on a less elaborate scale. The glory years of the antebellum South were gone forever.

The dawn of the twentieth century brought enormous improvements in labor-saving tools and packaged ingredients. Mechanical eggbeaters and flour sifters were early inventions that facilitated cake making, but, today, mixers and food processors make fast work of a job that formerly took all day. Baking powder, canned coconut, and condensed milk were greeted with joy by early twentieth century cooks who would be amazed by the number of ingredients that come in cans today. Perhaps the greatest boon to dessert makers was the invention of the modern refrigerator. Now, pies and molds can finish "cooking" without the cook's constant attention.

The great desserts of the South will always be vital elements of Southern hospitality. They are the logical endings to family dinners and the anticipated climax of elegant parties. They are as old-fashioned as ambrosia at Christmas and as up-to-date as America's current interest in back-to-basics cooking. No matter how homogeneous our society becomes, they will remain symbolic of the South.

THE 100 GREATEST DESSERTS OF THE SOUTH

CAKES

Cakes are the ultimate Southern dessert. The elegant creations are especially in evidence at Thanksgiving and Christmas when tables groan beneath platters of delicate Coconut Cake, crunchy Texas Toasted Pecan Cake, and rich Fruitcake. Cakes are important to other celebrations such as Mardi Gras when the colorful Kings' Cake plays an essential role in the festivities. The yeasty, ring-shaped dessert is decorated with sugar crystals tinted with brilliant carnival colors: purple, green, and gold. Traditionally, a bean or pecan half is tucked inside, and the finder is named king of the next party.

Cakes appear frequently throughout Southern history. George Washington's mother, Mary Ball Washington, was among our first cake-makers. She served fresh-baked gingerbread, accompanied by a glass of Madeira, to General Lafayette when he visited her at Fredericksburg. Showy Lord and Lady Baltimore Cakes are thought to have been named for the third Lord Baltimore and his Lady, who arrived in 1661 from England to govern the land which later became Maryland. Writer Owen Wister became so enamored with the taste of Lady Baltimore Cake that he named his novel *Lady Baltimore* in 1906. The moist, fruit-and-nut-filled Lane Cake, named for Emma Rylander Lane of Clayton, Alabama, became a sensation in 1898. Mrs. Lane published the recipe in her cookbook, *Some Good Things to Eat*. It has been called the "Southern Belle" of cakes.

Southerners are prone to associate cake making with love and friendly concern. We appear at our new neighbor's door with welcoming squares of Mississippi Mud, applaud a baby's arrival with slices of Hummingbird, cheer sick friends with soothing Lemon Cheese, and comfort grieving families with consoling Caramel. Whether the occasion is happy or sad, making someone a cake is a Southerner's way of saying, "I care."

CRIS BURNS' CARAMEL CAKE

The ultimate caramel cake with caramel icing

CARAMEL SYRUP
1 cup sugar
1 cup hot water

Melt sugar over medium heat in an iron skillet. Slowly add hot water and simmer 5 to 10 minutes, stirring occasionally with a wooden spoon.

1 cup butter (no substitute)	1 teaspoon vanilla
1$^{1}/_{2}$ cups sugar	6 tablespoons caramel
5 eggs, separated	syrup
2$^{1}/_{2}$ cups flour	3 teaspoons baking
$^{3}/_{4}$ cup milk	powder

Cream butter and sugar, saving 5 tablespoons of sugar for later use. Add beaten egg yolks. Mix in 2 cups flour alternately with milk. Beat well. Add vanilla and 6 tablespoons caramel syrup. Then add remaining $^{1}/_{2}$ cup flour and baking powder. Fold in egg whites, beaten with remaining 5 tablespoons of sugar. Bake in buttered tube pan 40 to 45 minutes in 325° oven until done.

ICING
2$^{1}/_{2}$ cups sugar	1 cup milk
1 stick butter	$^{1}/_{2}$ teaspoon vanilla

Combine sugar, butter, and milk in a saucepan. Place candy thermometer on pan. Cook over medium heat until it comes to a boil. Add remainder of caramel syrup and cook to the soft ball stage on candy thermometer. Remove from heat; cool; add vanilla. Beat with a hand mixer or wooden spoon until spreading consistency. If it gets too thick, add a little cream. Ice the cooled cake.

To grease pans, put butter in a small saucepan and place on the back of a warm stove. When melted, salt will settle to the bottom; butter is then clarified. Just before putting in batter, brush with butter, dredge pans thoroughly with flour, invert, and shake pan to remove all excess flour.

CAKES

CHOCOLATE–CHOCOLATE– CHOCOLATE CAKE

From the Pirate's House restaurant in Savannah, Georgia

$^3/_4$ cup butter
5 eggs, separated
$2^1/_2$ cups sugar
4 ounces unsweetened baking
  chocolate, melted

$2^1/_2$ cups sifted flour
1 teaspoon baking soda
1 cup buttermilk
1 teaspoon vanilla

Have butter and eggs at room temperature. Line bottoms of 3 8-inch round cake pans with wax paper; grease paper and flour. Preheat oven to 350°. Cream butter and sugar until light and fluffy. Beat in egg yolks one at a time; beat in melted chocolate. Sift flour and baking soda together. Beat in alternately with buttermilk, starting and ending with flour. Beat in vanilla. Beat egg whites until stiff but not dry. Beat one-fourth of the egg whites into chocolate mixture to lighten it, then fold chocolate mixture into egg whites gently but thoroughly. The chocolate batter will be very heavy and won't want to cooperate, but be firm. Divide batter among pans; smooth tops and bake for 30 to 35 minutes, until tops spring back when lightly touched and cakes shrink from sides of pans. Cool on wire racks and turn out. You may have to slip a finger under the wax paper to get it started. Fill and ice. Serves 12 or more.

FILLING

$^1/_2$ cup sugar
3 tablespoons flour
Pinch of salt
1 egg

2 ounces unsweetened chocolate, melted
1 cup milk
1 tablespoon butter
$^1/_2$ teaspoon vanilla extract

Mix dry ingredients. Whisk in egg until smooth. Melt chocolate in milk in a heavy saucepan, stirring constantly.

Gradually pour milk into egg mixture, whisking rapidly and constantly. Return mixture to saucepan and cook, stirring constantly with a wooden spoon, until mixture thickens and comes to a boil. Remove from heat; beat in butter and vanilla. Pour into a bowl, place a piece of plastic wrap directly on the surface of the filling, and refrigerate until cool. Use between layers of cake.

ICING

2 ounces unsweetened baking chocolate	1 cup milk
	2 cups sugar
1/3 cup butter	1 teaspoon vanilla extract
1 teaspoon flour	

Melt chocolate and butter in a large, heavy saucepan over low heat, stirring constantly. Dissolve flour in part of the milk; add milk, flour and sugar to chocolate, bring to a boil, stirring frequently, and boil until mixture reaches soft ball stage on a candy thermometer (234°). Remove from heat, stir in vanilla, and beat with an electric mixer until icing becomes just thick enough to spread. Do not let it harden too much. If icing does become too hard, beat in a little milk. Ice entire outside of cake. Dip spatula or knife in hot water to smooth icing.

Note: Don't let the length of this recipe intimidate you. For true chocolate lovers, it is well worth the effort.

This recipe is from the Pirate's House in Savannah, Georgia. The restaurant is located in a building, which was originally an inn for visiting seamen, and was built in the mid-1700s. It is recognized by the American Museum Society as an authentic house museum.

WHITE CHOCOLATE CAKE
A sumptuous cake with White Chocolate Icing

$^3/_4$ cup white chocolate,
   coarsely chopped
$^1/_2$ cup hot water
1 cup (2 sticks) butter, room
   temperature
$1^1/_2$ cups sugar
3 eggs
$2^1/_2$ cups flour

1 teaspoon baking soda
$^1/_2$ teaspoon baking powder
$^1/_2$ teaspoon salt
1 cup buttermilk
1 teaspoon vanilla
$^1/_2$ cup pecans, chopped
$^1/_2$ cup flaked coconut

Melt white chocolate in hot water in top of a double boiler. Mix butter and sugar until a light lemon color. Add eggs one at a time and beat well after each addition. Sift flour, baking soda, baking powder, and salt. Add the dry ingredients to the butter-sugar-egg mixture, adding buttermilk alternately with dry ingredients. Add chocolate and vanilla. Beat 3 to 5 minutes at medium setting. Stir in pecans and coconut. Pour batter into 2 greased and floured 9-inch pans. Bake for 30 to 35 minutes at 350° or until top springs back when touched with fingers. Remove from oven. Cool 30 minutes. Run a knife around the edges of the pan and carefully remove layer cakes from pans. Allow to cool completely.

WHITE CHOCOLATE ICING

$^3/_4$ cup white chocolate,
   coarsely chopped
$2^1/_2$ teaspoons flour
1 cup milk
1 cup (2 sticks) butter, room
   temperature

1 cup sugar
$1^1/_2$ teaspoons vanilla
$^1/_2$ cup flaked coconut

In a saucepan set in hot water, melt white chocolate and add flour. Blend. Add milk and blend. Stir constantly until mixture thickens. Cool. Cream butter, sugar, and vanilla. Beat 2 to 3 minutes and gradually add cooled chocolate mixture. Beat at high speed with an electric mixer. Icing should be of the consistency of whipped cream. Stack cake layers with bottoms toward each other. Ice bottom layer and sides and top of the cake. Sprinkle coconut over icing. Serves 12 to 14.

To cream, use a wooden spoon, working mixture with a gliding motion between the back of the spoon and the side of the bowl, in short strokes. It should become light in color and even, smooth, and creamy in texture. If it becomes curdled and frothy, you have worked it too long and it will result in a coarsely grained cake.

CAKES

TEXAS CANDY CAKE

People who do not like fruitcake love this cake

½ pound chopped candied red cherries
½ pound chopped candied pineapple
½ pound chopped dates
1 tablespoon flour
4⅓ cups chopped pecans
4 ounces flaked coconut
1 14-ounce can sweetened condensed milk

Mix the chopped fruit with the tablespoon of flour. Stir in the chopped pecans, flaked coconut, and the can of condensed milk. Preheat the oven to 250°. Grease and flour a tube pan. Press mixture into pan and bake 1½ hours. Allow the cake to cool and wrap tightly in cheesecloth. Refrigerate at least 2 weeks. Makes about 24 thin slices.

Dip small pieces or squares of angel food cake into Seven-Minute Frosting (see Old-Fashioned Coconut Cake for recipe) and roll in coconut for party snowballs.

NATCHEZ CHRISTMAS CAKE

From Bobby J. Potter at the Post House Restaurant in Natchez, Mississippi

1 15-ounce package golden raisins
1 15-ounce package currants
1 fifth bourbon
1¹/₂ (3 sticks) cups butter
2 cups sugar
1 dozen eggs
1 cup wild plum jelly
2 pints preserves, cut and drained (strawberry, fig, pear, or blackberry)
1 teaspoon soda
1 cup Louisiana molasses
4 cups whole wheat flour
1 teaspoon allspice

1 teaspoon mace
1 teaspoon black pepper
2 teaspoons cloves
2 teaspoons cinnamon
3 cups pecans, chopped
¹/₂ pound lemon peel, chopped
¹/₂ pound orange peel, chopped
4 ounces candied ginger
1 pound chopped candied dates or figs
1 pound chopped candied pineapple
1 pound chopped candied apricots

Cake should be made 4 to 6 weeks in advance. Reduce ginger by half if you use it earlier. Three hours before starting, empty raisins and currants into a saucepan and pour all but 1 cup bourbon over. Simmer over low heat until they are puffed, stirring every 20 minutes. Cream butter and sugar, adding eggs one at a time, beating well. Add jelly and preserves. Mix soda into the molasses. When doubled in size and light brown in color, add to batter. Using reserved bourbon, rinse out molasses jar and add to batter. To the flour, in a separate bowl, add seasonings and thoroughly dredge all nuts and fruits (except raisins and currants). When thoroughly dredged, and using all flour from dredging process, add fruit and nuts to the batter. It is best to put the dredged fruit and nuts in a large preserving kettle and add batter to it. Stir thoroughly. Then add puffed raisins and currants and any bourbon residue that may be left. Prepare 2 tube pans or 4 loaf pans. Line with greased brown paper. Pour in batter and bake at 275° for 2 hours. Remove from oven and soak cakes with bourbon—all they will hold. When cool, wrap and store 4 to 6 weeks before cutting. Makes 2 tube cakes or 4 loaf cakes.

When a cake is done it should be cooled in the pan on a rack, for about 5 minutes, and then cooled out of the pan, on a rack, until all heat has left. There are a few exceptions which a recipe will point out.

CANDY BAR CAKE
Candy is not one of the ingredients—the cake is similar to a famous candy bar

2 cups sugar	**FILLING**
1 cup margarine	1 cup sugar
5 eggs	1 cup evaporated milk
1 cup all-purpose flour	16 ounces coconut
1 cup self-rising flour	12 large marshmallows
1 cup milk	1 teaspoon vanilla
1 teaspoon vanilla	

Cream sugar and margarine together. Beat eggs into the mixture one at a time. Sift the two flours together, add alternately with the milk. Stir the vanilla in the mixture and pour batter into 3 greased and floured 8-inch pans. Bake at 350° for 30 minutes.

It is important to prepare the filling while the cake is baking. The cake should be stacked while it is still warm and the filling is still hot. The heat holds the layers together. Put sugar and milk in a saucepan and bring to a boil. Add coconut and marshmallows. Stir and cook for 5 minutes. Add vanilla. Spread between cake layers as you remove layers from the pans. Do not put any on the top layer; it will be frosted.

FROSTING

2 cups sugar	¹/₂ cup butter
¹/₂ cup cocoa	¹/₂ cup milk

Combine ingredients and, stirring constantly, bring to a boil. Boil hard for 2 minutes. Remove from heat and beat until thick enough to spread. Frost cake. Serves 16.

JUDY BLACKBURN'S WALNUT CREAM CAKE

Grand prize winner in a recipe contest

5 extra-large eggs, separated
2 cups sugar, divided
$^1/_2$ cup butter
$^1/_2$ cup margarine
$^1/_2$ teaspoon salt
$1^1/_2$ teaspoons vanilla

1 teaspoon baking soda
1 cup buttermilk
2 cups flour
1 cup walnuts, finely chopped
1 can ($3^1/_2$ ounces) flaked
   coconut

Have all ingredients at room temperature. Beat egg whites until they form soft peaks. Add $^1/_2$ cup sugar slowly; beat until like meringue. Cream butter, margarine, remaining sugar, salt, and vanilla. Add egg yolks one at a time. Stir baking soda into buttermilk. Alternately add the buttermilk and flour to the butter mixture. Start and finish with flour. Fold in egg white mixture, then walnuts, then coconut. Bake in 3 9-inch greased and floured pans at 325° for about 40 minutes. Cool. Ice layers and sides with icing. Keeps well in refrigerator. Serves 12 or more.

ICING

$1^1/_2$ sticks butter
$1^1/_2$ 8-ounce packages cream
   cheese

$1^1/_2$ boxes confectioners'
   sugar
$1^1/_2$ teaspoons vanilla

Beat all ingredients until consistency of whipped cream. Ice cake; decorate top with a ring of chopped nuts.

Judy Blackburn won a Grand Prize in the 1984 Clarion-Ledger/Jackson Daily News (Jackson, Mississippi) Cookbook Contest for her Walnut Cream Cake.

CAKES

BARBARA'S KING CAKE
This version is a real winner!

1 cup milk
$^1/_2$ cup butter or margarine
$^1/_2$ cup sugar plus 1 tablespoon
1 teaspoon salt
4 large eggs, beaten

Grated rind of 1 lemon or
   orange
$^1/_4$ cup warm water
2 packages dry yeast
$4^1/_2$ cups bread flour
$^1/_4$ cup oil

FILLING
1 stick butter or margarine,
   softened
$^1/_2$ cup brown sugar

$^1/_2$ cup granulated sugar
2 tablespoons cinnamon (or
   to taste)

Scald milk (microwave about 5 minutes on high or you may use a pot on top of stove). To scalded milk add butter or margarine and $^1/_2$ cup of sugar. The hot milk will melt the butter and dissolve the sugar. Add salt, beaten eggs, and grated rind. Stir gently. To $^1/_4$ cup warm water add the extra tablespoon of sugar and the yeast. The sugar will cause the yeast mixture to foam; this proves the yeast is active. After yeast is thoroughly dissolved, add to cooled milk mixture. Add flour 1 cup at a time, mixing thoroughly after each addition. The dough will be very sticky and soft. The soft dough makes for a light texture of the cake. Drizzle the oil around the side of your mixing bowl. At this point you may have to use your hands to mix the dough. Roll the dough around the bowl, greasing the sides of the bowl with the oil. Cover the bowl with a damp towel. Allow to rise until dough has doubled in volume, approximately 3 hours. After rising, punch dough down and knead on a floured board gently for about 2 minutes. This amount of dough will make 1 large King Cake or may be split to make 2 smaller cakes.

Roll dough on a well-floured board into a large rectangle, rolling the dough as thin as possible without tearing it. Spread dough rectangle with softened butter. Mix brown and granulated sugar and cinnamon together. Sprinkle over entire rectangle, spreading it evenly. Cut rectangle into thirds (a pizza cutter gives you a nice clean cut). Roll each third of dough like a jelly roll. Stretch rolls to give you 3 equal lengths. Braid the 3 strips and shape into a ring on a greased baking sheet. If you cover your baking sheet with a heavy duty foil and then grease, it makes the cake easier to handle after baking. Let braided ring rise 1$^1/_2$ to 2 hours. Bake at 375° in a preheated oven for about 20 minutes, or until brown.

ICING

3 cups confectioners' sugar
$^1/_2$ stick butter or margarine, softened
$^1/_2$ teaspoon vanilla extract
$^1/_4$ cup milk
Juice from the grated fruit

Colored sugar (dye sugar with food coloring: purple, gold, and green)
1 plastic baby (if baby unavailable you may use a pinto bean)

After baking, hide the baby or bean in baked cake, inserting from underneath. Make icing while cake cools. Mix icing ingredients together, except for colored sugar. The icing should be the consistency of pancake batter. After cake is cooled ice cake and decorate with colored sugar. Slice, serve, and enjoy. As the tradition goes, the person who gets the slice with the baby must provide the next King Cake.

This recipe comes from Barbara Schwegmann, a nurse in Marrero, Louisiana.

KINGS' CAKE

Celebrate Mardi Gras with the purple, green, and gold Gâteau des Rois or "Kings' Cake"

1 package yeast	1 dried bean
1/4 cup warm water	3 cups granulated sugar
6 tablespoons milk	2 to 3 drops purple food
4 cups flour	coloring
1 cup (2 sticks) butter	2 to 3 drops green food
3/4 cup sugar	coloring
1/4 teaspoon salt	2 to 3 drops yellow food
4 eggs	coloring
Melted butter	White corn syrup

Dissolve yeast in warm water. Add milk that has been scalded and cooled. Mix in 1/2 cup of the flour to make a soft dough. In a separate bowl, combine butter, 3/4 cup sugar, salt, and eggs. Mix well and add soft ball of yeast dough. Mix thoroughly. Gradually blend in 2 1/2 cups of flour to make a medium dough. Place in a greased bowl and brush top of dough with the melted butter. Cover with a damp cloth and let it rise until doubled in bulk, about 3 hours. Use remaining 1 cup flour to knead dough and to roll into a "rope" of dough. Place on a large greased cookie sheet and shape "rope" into a circle, connecting ends of dough by dampening with water. Cover with a damp cloth and let rise until doubled in bulk, about 1 hour. A bean may be placed in the cake at this point, if desired. Bake in a preheated 325° oven for 35 to 45 minutes, or until lightly browned. Decorate by coloring the sugar, 2 to 3 drops of each color to 1 cup of sugar. To achieve a gold color you may add a tiny drop of red to the yellow food color. Brush the top of the cake with corn syrup and alternate 3-inch bands of purple, green, and gold colored sugar. Serves 16 to 24.

Note: If you wish to mail the cake, place it in a large

plastic zip-lock bag. Place the bag in a box filled with unsalted popped pop corn.

The Gâteau des Rois or "Kings' Cake" is inseparably connected with Mardi Gras—New Orleans and carnival season. The most famous of the Creole desserts, the "Kings' Cake" evolved from the Creole custom of choosing a king and queen on the Twelfth Night (January 6), the feast day that commemorates the visit of the three Wise Men of the East to the Christ Child in Bethlehem. The method of choosing a king was cutting the Kings' Cake and serving each person present a piece of the cake with a glass of champagne. Cleverly hidden within the cake was a bean. If the finder of the bean was a lady, she chose her king by presenting to him a bunch of violets. If the finder was a gentleman, he would choose his queen by offering her the flower in his lapel and would then escort her around the parlor in le tour de salon. Ever since those early days, during the period between January 6 and Mardi Gras, a king and queen were chosen for the occasion in this manner, and a new royal pair was chosen every week thereafter until Mardi Gras.

CAKES

RED VELVET CAKE

From Shirley McConnell—a food specialist
from Pensacola, Florida

1 1/2 cups sugar
1/2 cup shortening
2 eggs
2 cups flour
1 tablespoon cocoa
1 teaspoon salt

1 cup buttermilk
1 teaspoon vanilla
2 ounces red food coloring
1 teaspoon soda
1 tablespoon vinegar

Cream sugar and shortening. Add eggs and beat well. Sift flour, cocoa, and salt three times and add alternately to creamed mixture with buttermilk. Add vanilla and food coloring. Dissolve soda in vinegar; fold it into the cake (do not beat). Bake in 2 greased and floured 9-inch cake pans at 350° for 25 to 30 minutes or until cake-tester comes out clean. Turn cake out on a rack; cool and frost. Will serve 12.

FROSTING

1/4 cup flour
1 cup milk
1/4 teaspoon salt
1 cup butter

1 cup confectioners' sugar
2 teaspoons vanilla
1 cup chopped pecans

Mix flour, milk, and salt in a blender until smooth. Cook slowly until very thick. Cool completely. Cream butter and sugar until fluffy. Beat in vanilla. Add to cooled mixture and beat well. Frost the cake and garnish with pecans.

During the late 1920s or early 1930s a Southern lady is said to have eaten at the Waldorf Astoria. She especially enjoyed this cake and requested the recipe. At the end of the meal she was presented with the recipe and a bill for a large sum of money. She paid it and graciously shared the recipe along with the joke on herself with friends. Now it is one of the South's favorite desserts.

OLD–FASHIONED COCONUT CAKE
A classic

2¹/₄ cups sifted flour
1¹/₂ teaspoons baking
   powder
¹/₂ teaspoon baking soda
³/₄ teaspoon salt
¹/₂ cup unsalted butter

1 ¹/₄ cups sugar
3 eggs
¹/₂ cup angel flake coconut
1¹/₄ cups buttermilk
1¹/₂ teaspoons vanilla
Coconut

Sift together the dry ingredients. Cream butter and sugar. Add the eggs one at a time to the creamed mixture. Beat well after each addition. Combine the ¹/₂ cup coconut and the buttermilk. Add alternately with flour mixture to sugar mixture (on slow speed if using mixer). Add vanilla. Pour into 2 greased and floured 9-inch cake pans. Bake at 375° for 25 to 30 minutes. This can be made in 3 layers with the cooking time shortened. Serves 12 or more.

FILLING

2 egg whites
¹/₂ cup nonalcoholic pina colada
mix

1¹/₂ cups angel flake coconut
4 tablespoons confectioners'
   sugar

Beat egg whites until stiff. Add other ingredients to egg whites. Mix gently with spoon. Do not cook. Spread between cake layers. Ice cake with Seven-Minute Frosting. Sprinkle cake with coconut.

SEVEN-MINUTE FROSTING

1 1/2 cups egg whites, room temperature

1/4 teaspoon salt

1 1/4 teaspoons cream of tartar

1 1/2 cups sugar, sifted

3/4 teaspoon vanilla

3/4 teaspoon almond flavoring

1 cup flour, sifted

Combine ingredients in top of double boiler. Beat well. Place over simmering water. Cook, beating constantly at high speed with an electric hand mixer about 7 minutes or until it is triple in volume and holds firm peaks. Remove from heat.

This wonderful recipe was contributed by Nancy Calhoun, vice-president of Pelican Publishing Company in Gretna, Louisiana.

To crack a coconut, puncture the eyes at the end of the coconut and drain off liquid. Place in a 350° oven for 30 minutes. Place hot coconut on a hard surface and hit hard with a hammer; pry out meat with an old table knife, remove brown skin with a potato peeler, rinse, and dry on paper towels. One coconut will provide 3 to 4 cups meat. To grate in a blender or food processor, cut into 1/2-inch cubes and drop in 1 cup at a time.

COCONUT CAKE (BASIC 1–2–3–4 CAKE)

Tall and showy with lemon and raspberry filling

3 cups cake flour, sifted
2 teaspoons baking powder
$^1/_2$ teaspoon salt
1 cup butter or margarine, softened
2 cups sugar
4 eggs
1 teaspoon vanilla

1 cup milk
1 cup raspberry jam
1 recipe Lemon Cheese Cake filling (see index)
1 recipe Seven-Minute Frosting (see index)
1 cup flaked coconut (freshly grated, if possible)

Sift together cake flour, baking powder, and salt. Set aside. Cream butter and sugar; add eggs and vanilla; beat at high speed for 3 minutes. Add flour mixture alternately with milk, at low speed on mixer. Scrape sides of bowl with rubber spatula after each addition. Pour batter into 3 greased and floured 8-inch cake pans. Bake at 350° for 30 minutes or until the centers spring back when lightly pressed with fingertip. Cool layers in the pans on wire racks 10 minutes. Turn out onto racks. Cool thoroughly. Spread raspberry jam thinly over two layers. Spoon and smooth lemon cheese filling over jam. Stack, ending with plain layer. Frost sides and top with Seven-Minute Frosting. Sprinkle with coconut. Serves 12 or more.

WINIFRED CHENEY'S BLACK-BERRY JAM CAKE

Winifred Green Cheney is one of the South's most noted food writers

1 cup butter, softened
2 cups sugar, sifted
4 large eggs, room temperature
3 cups cake flour, measured
   after sifting
3 teaspoons baking powder
1 teaspoon ground cinnamon

$^1/_8$ teaspoon salt
1 teaspoon ground cloves
1 cup milk
1 teaspoon lemon extract
1 teaspoon grated lemon rind
1 cup fairly firm blackberry
   jam, preferably seedless.

In a large bowl, cream butter and sugar until light and fluffy. Add eggs one at a time; beat well. If using an electric mixer, place butter, sugar, and 2 eggs in a large, deep bowl and beat 4 minutes at high speed. Add remaining 2 eggs, one at a time, and beat well. Sift flour, baking powder, cinnamon, salt, and cloves together three times. Add flour mixture to creamed mixture alternately with milk, a small amount each time, ending with flour mixture. Beat well. Add lemon extract and rind, then jam. Spoon batter into 3 greased and floured layer pans. Bake in a preheated 350° oven for 20 to 25 minutes until cake tests done. Cool on wire rack for 15 minutes. If making cake for a party, use two batches of icing—one for putting between the layers, the other for top and sides of cake. Makes 3 9-inch layers (serves 14 to 16).

NEVER FAIL WHITE ICING

3 medium-size or large eggs,
   whites only
$^1/_4$ teaspoon cream of tartar
$1^1/_2$ cups sifted sugar

5 tablespoons cold water
$1^1/_2$ teaspoons light corn
   syrup
1 teaspoon vanilla extract

Place all ingredients with exception of vanilla in top of a double boiler over rapidly boiling water. Beat mixture with electric mixer at high speed. You may use a rotary beater or

36

wire whisk, but the electric mixer makes it easier. Cut down mixture from sides of pan with spatula as it cooks. Beat constantly about 7 minutes or until icing will stand in peaks and has attained a high gloss. Remove icing from heat and add vanilla. Center a layer of cake on cake plate and put 5 heaping tablespoons of icing in a circle on top and gently spread toward the sides. Use a dinner knife or a 1-inch wide spatula for spreading. Position top cake layer and repeat icing method. To ice the sides apply a tablespoon of icing at top of side, working it down as you go around the cake. Repeat until cake is completely covered. Make icing for sides and tops of 2 (8-inch) layers.

Winifred Green Cheney, noted Southern food writer and hostess, has authored two cookbooks, Cooking for Company *and* The Southern Hospitality Cookbook. *The latter was selected by the American Book Publishing Association as one of 250 best books in America and as a result is included in the White House Library. The Jam Cake is from* The Southern Hospitality Cookbook *and is reprinted with the permission of Oxmoor House, Inc.*

TEXAS TOASTED PECAN CAKE

The Deep South's favorite nut in an unforgettable cake

4 tablespoons butter	2 eggs
1½ cups pecans, chopped	2 cups flour
¾ cup butter	2 teaspoons baking powder
1⅓ cups sugar	¼ teaspoon salt
1½ teaspoons vanilla	⅔ cup milk

Melt 4 tablespoons butter in a baking pan in the oven at 350°. Add pecans and toast 10 to 15 minutes. Cream ¾ cup butter; gradually add sugar; beat until fluffy. Add vanilla. Beat in eggs, one at a time. Sift together flour, baking powder, and salt. Add to creamed mixture alternately with milk. Beat after each addition. Fold in 1 cup pecans. Set aside remaining ½ cup pecans for top of cake. Bake at 350° in greased and floured pans for 30 to 35 minutes. Cool completely before icing.

FROSTING

6 tablespoons butter	1 teaspoon vanilla
3 cups powdered sugar	3-4 tablespoons light cream

Cream butter. Add powdered sugar gradually. Add vanilla and cream. Beat until smooth. Spread frosting between layers and on cake. Sprinkle remaining pecans atop cake. Serves 12.

HUMMINGBIRD CAKE
Cinnamon, fruit, and nuts create a spicy flavor

3 cups all-purpose flour
2 cups sugar
1 teaspoon salt
1 teaspoon cinnamon
1 teaspoon soda
3 eggs, beaten

1 cup salad oil
$1^1/_2$ teaspoons vanilla
1 can (8-ounce) crushed
  pineapple, undrained
1 cup pecans, chopped
2 bananas, mashed with fork

Combine the dry ingredients in a bowl. Stir in eggs and salad oil until dry ingredients are moistened, but do not overbeat. Add vanilla, crushed pineapple, pecans, and bananas and stir well. Pour batter into 3 well-greased and floured 8-inch cake pans. Bake at 350° for 25 to 30 minutes or until cake tests done. Cool cake in pans for 10 minutes, remove from pans to racks, and cool thoroughly before icing.

FROSTING

8 ounces cream cheese, softened
1 cup butter or margarine,
  softened

$1^3/_4$ pounds confectioners'
  sugar
2 teaspoons vanilla
1 cup pecans, chopped

Mix cream cheese and butter together and cream until smooth. Add powdered sugar slowly and beat until light and fluffy. Add vanilla. Spread between layers and on top and sides of cake. Sprinkle with pecans. Serves 12.

SWEET POTATO PUDDING CAKE WITH BOURBON–PECAN TOPPING

This Deep-South pudding cake may also be served with Bourbon Caramel Sauce

1¹/₂ cups flour, sifted
¹/₄ teaspoon salt
2 teaspoons baking powder
¹/₂ cup margarine
2 eggs, beaten
³/₄ cup sugar
1 teaspoon nutmeg

1 teaspoon cinnamon
2 cups hot sweet potatoes, mashed
¹/₂ cup milk
1 tablespoon lemon juice
¹/₄ cup bourbon, warmed

Combine flour, salt, and baking powder; sift. Add margarine, eggs, sugar, nutmeg, and cinnamon to hot mashed sweet potatoes. Beat thoroughly. Add flour and milk alternately. Beat well after each addition. Add lemon juice. Grease a loaf pan and pour mixture into it. Bake in a 350° oven for 1 hour to 1 hour and 20 minutes or until a knife inserted in the center comes out clean. Remove from the oven and immediately punch holes in the top of the cake with toothpick or ice pick. Brush top with the warmed bourbon. Make the topping and spoon over the pudding cake while still in the pan. To serve, cut cake down the middle and then slice crosswise. Pudding cake may be served with Bourbon Caramel Sauce (see Heavenly Surprise Dessert for recipe), if desired.

BOURBON PECAN TOPPING

¹/₂ cup (1 stick) butter
¹/₂ cup brown sugar, packed
¹/₄ cup cream

¹/₄ cup bourbon
1 cup coconut
1 cup pecans, chopped

Melt butter. Add sugar and cream. Stir in the bourbon. Bring to a boil and boil 3 minutes. Cool and beat until it thickens. Add coconut and pecans. Pour over cake and run under the broiler until it bubbles. Serves 16.

VICKSBURG PRUNE CAKE

Moist and flavorful—this recipe is one of the best

3 eggs
1 cup vegetable oil
1¹/₂ cups sugar
2 cups flour
1 teaspoon soda
1 teaspoon cinnamon
1 teaspoon allspice

1 teaspoon nutmeg
1 teaspoon salt
1 cup buttermilk
1 cup cooked pitted prunes,
   cut up
1 cup chopped nuts (optional)

Mix all cake ingredients in order given. It is best to sift all dry ingredients together before adding to mixture. Grease and flour a large baking pan 10 x 14 inches or larger. Pour in cake batter and bake at 350° about 40 minutes. Remove from oven and immediately prick all over top with a knife or fork before pouring icing over cake. Serves 12.

ICING

1 cup sugar
¹/₂ cup buttermilk
1 teaspoon soda

1 tablespoon dark corn syrup
¹/₂ cup butter or margarine
Whipped cream (optional)

Mix all ingredients, except whipped cream, in a boiler and bring to a rolling boil. Remove from heat and beat slightly. While still very warm, pour over hot cake which has been pricked. Serve with whipped cream if desired.

This recipe is from Mrs. George Jabour, Sr., and is used with the permission of the Vintage Vicksburg Cookbook committee.

GENERAL ROBERT E. LEE ORANGE–LEMON CAKE

Mouth-watering cake from Kentucky's Beaumont Inn

2 cups cake flour (sift twice
   before measuring)
1½ teaspoons baking powder
½ teaspoon cream of tartar
2 cups sugar (sift six times)
½ cup salad oil

1 lemon (juice and grated
   yellow
of rind)
9 eggs, separated
A few grains of salt

Sift cake flour, baking powder, and cream of tartar together six times. Stir in sugar. Pour salad oil over these ingredients and mix well. Stir in lemon juice and rind. Beat egg yolks in electric mixer, add salad oil mixture, and blend well. Add salt to egg whites and beat until stiff. Combine with egg yolk mixture. Grease 4 9-inch cake pans; divide batter among them equally and bake at 325° for 20 minutes. Turn cake upside down on rack until cool. There will be 4 thin layers. Serves 12 or more.

ORANGE–LEMON FROSTING

2 pounds confectioners' sugar
½ cup butter, softened
4 tablespoons lemon juice
6-8 tablespoons orange juice
   (enough to make frosting
   easy to spread)

3 egg yolks
Rind of 2 lemons (yellow
   only), grated
Rind of 4 oranges, grated

Cream sugar and butter. Gradually beat in juices, then egg yolks. Mix in rinds. Ice cake. This cake should be refrigerated in a tight container due to icing being uncooked.

The Beaumont Inn in Harrodsburg, deep in the heart of Bluegrass country, is a former girls' school which has been converted into a lovely inn. Famous for the delicious Southern food served in its dining room, the inn is over one hundred years old.

For separating eggs, paper cups are handy to have on hand. Separate the eggs into them and store what is not needed with a plastic covering.

CAKES

LANE CAKE
Tall and showy with a rich nut and fruit filling

1 cup butter, softened	¹/₂ teaspoon salt
2 cups sugar	1 cup milk
4 cups cake flour, sifted	8 egg whites, stiffly beaten
2 teaspoons baking powder	1 teaspoon vanilla

Cream butter, add sugar slowly, and mix well. Sift dry ingredients and add alternately with milk. Fold in egg whites and add vanilla. Bake in 3 8-inch greased and floured cake pans at 350° for 30 minutes, or until a wooden pick inserted in center comes out clean. Cool in pans 10 minutes; remove from pans, and cool completely. Serves 10 or more.

FILLING

8 egg yolks	1 cup maraschino cherries,
1 cup sugar	chopped
1 stick butter, softened	1 cup raisins
1 cup pecans, chopped	1 cup grated coconut
	2 tablespoons bourbon

Beat egg yolks until light. Beat in sugar and butter. Cook in a double boiler over medium heat until thick. Stir in remaining ingredients. Cool. Spread between layers. Frost sides and top with Seven-Minute Frosting (see Old-Fashioned Coconut Cake for recipe).

Lane Cake was named for Emma Rylander Lane of Dayton, Alabama, who published it in her cookbook Some Good Things to Eat *(1898). Mrs. Lane thought the flavor improved if it were made several days before serving-giving the fruit and nuts time to mellow with the bourbon.*

LADY BALTIMORE CAKE

A novel was named for this cake

1 cup butter	1 cup milk
2 cups sifted sugar	2 teaspoons vanilla
3^1/$_2$ cups sifted cake flour	^{1}/$_2$ teaspoon almond extract
4 teaspoons baking powder	8 egg whites
^{1}/$_4$ teaspoon salt	

Cream butter and sugar until light. Add flour, sifted with baking powder and salt, alternately with milk. Beat well after each addition. Add extracts. Beat egg whites until stiff and fold into the mixture. Bake in 3 8-inch, well-greased layer pans at 350° for about 30 minutes. Cool in pans on racks for 10 minutes. Invert layers onto racks to finish cooling.

LADY BALTIMORE ICING

3 egg whites, unbeaten	1 teaspoon vanilla
2^1/$_4$ cups sugar	^{1}/$_2$ cup raisins, finely chopped
^{1}/$_2$ cup cold water	1 cup pecans, finely chopped
2 teaspoons light corn syrup	6 dried figs, finely chopped

Place egg whites, sugar, water, and corn syrup in top of a double boiler. Cook over boiling water, beating constantly for 7 minutes. Remove from heat, add vanilla, and blend well. Reserve one-half of icing for top and sides of cake. To the remainder add finely chopped raisins, pecans, and figs. Spread the two bottom layers with this filling and cover the top and sides with plain icing. Serves about 10.

Lady Baltimore Cake was immortalized by novelist Owen Wister, who was served a piece by a Charleston lady named Alicia Rhett Mayberry. The writer was so taken with the cake that he not only described it in his next novel, but named the book, published in 1906, Lady Baltimore.

SAM LITZENBERG'S WORLD FAMOUS CHEESECAKE

The Hungry Potter Restaurant in Marshall, Texas ships this cheesecake all over the world

$1/2$ cup graham cracker crumbs
$1/2$ teaspoon nutmeg
$1/2$ teaspoon cinnamon
40 ounces (5 8-ounce bricks) cream cheese, room temperature

$1^1/_2$ cups sugar
1 cup sour cream
1 teaspoon vanilla extract
6 large whole eggs, plus 3 egg yolks
1 tablespoon lemon zest

Coat the inside of a 10-inch springform pan with a food release product. Mix the graham cracker crumbs with nutmeg and cinnamon. Cover bottom of pan with the mixture. Pat it smooth with a spoon, covering bottom evenly. The seam where the side meets the bottom should be covered. Place cream cheese in a mixing bowl, one stick at a time, and blend until smooth. Add sugar and blend again. Add sour cream, mixing well. Scrape sides and bottom of the bowl with a spatula. Add vanilla, eggs, and lemon zest. Mix a few minutes to remove any lumps. To prevent batter from splattering and ruining the crust, place spatula in the bowl and lean it against the side. Pour batter onto the blade. Fill pan until you have $1/2$ inch of pan left showing. Using a toothpick, pop any bubbles in the batter. Preheat oven to 350°. Place cake in the center on middle rack. Remove top rack from oven. Close oven door and turn heat down to 325°. Bake 1 hour or until a light crust has formed on top of cake. Cake will rise and be over edge of pan. Reduce heat to 200° and bake 1 more hour. Turn oven off and allow the cake to stay in the oven until cool enough to touch. The center of cake should be firm and should have come back into pan. Chill overnight before serving. Serves 16.

CAKES

VARIATIONS

Other flavors: To add any of the many spirits that are so much fun to work with, pour them into the batter and mix. Start off with $^1/_2$ cup and taste. Add more if you wish but do not add more than 1 cup (8 ounces) or the cake will be too moist.

Amaretto Cheesecake: It will take more than 1 cup of Amaretto to get the proper flavor. Therefore, mix 2 tablespoons almond extract, 1 tablespoon vanilla extract, and 2 teaspoons chocolate extract to your cheesecake batter in place of the vanilla. This will give you that wonderful amaretto flavor without all of the extra liquid.

Lemon Cheesecake: Add $^1/_2$ cup fresh lemon juice and 1 tablespoon of lemon zest. Bake as directed.

Pumpkin Cheesecake: Make batter as for plain cheesecake. Before placing on the crust remove $1^1/_4$ cups of batter and add 10 ounces pumpkin and 1 tablespoon of pumpkin pie spices to remaining batter. Blend together and bake as directed.

Chocolate Swirl Cheesecake: In a small mixing bowl pour 2 cups of the cheesecake batter. Whisk in $^1/_2$ can of your favorite chocolate syrup. Mix until it is a dark brown. To pour batter use the spatula as you did for plain cheesecake. Stop at about halfway. Pour half of the chocolate mixture into the pan and pour in a circle around the side of the pan. With a fork swirl the chocolate batter around. Do no go too deep and disturb the crust. Pour in the rest of the plain batter leaving enough room in the pan for the rest of the chocolate mix. Pour in the chocolate mixture and swirl it with a fork again. Swirl in circles and make little designs in it. Don't overdo. Bake as you would the plain cheesecake.

PRALINE CHEESECAKE

5 8-ounce bricks cream cheese	2 tablespoons vanilla extract
1³/₄ cups brown sugar, packed	6 whole eggs, plus 3 yolks
2 cups sour cream	1 cup pecans

Use the same crust as the original recipe. Proceed with cream cheese. Add sugar and sour cream. Add vanilla.

Break your eggs into your blender or food processor. Add pecans and turn it on. Process or blend until the pecans are dust in the fluid. Pour into the bowl with the cream cheese. The rest of the directions are the same. The batter will be a bit thinner because of the added water in the brown sugar. If you add enough pecans it will make up for this. Bake as instructed. Serve the cake with a spoonful of pecan praline sauce over it.

PECAN PRALINE SAUCE

1 cup heavy cream	2¹/₂ cups brown sugar
1 cup pecans, chopped	¹/₄ teaspoon salt
¹/₂ cup butter (1 stick)	2 tablespoons vanilla

Pour cream into a blender and run on low. Slowly add the pecans into the blender to grind them. Set aside. In a large pot, melt butter over high heat. Add brown sugar and salt. Whisk with wire whisk. When it starts to bubble well, add cream and pecan mixture. Keep whisking until well mixed and uniform in color. Reduce heat to medium, stirring constantly. Cook for 5 more minutes, stirring. Remove from heat, add vanilla, and allow to cool. Place in a container and refrigerate. To serve, place a spoonful in a skillet and heat. You may adjust flavor a bit by adding an ounce of bourbon along with the vanilla. The sauce is excellent over praline cheesecake, bread pudding, or ice cream. Makes about 2¹/₂ cups.

To test a cake for doneness, insert a wire cake-tester or a toothpick (broom straws may also be used). It will emerge clean when the cake is done. Cake should be lightly browned and beginning to shrink from the sides of the pan.

CANDY AND CONFECTIONS

The art of candy making is nearly as old as recorded history; references were found in Egyptian papyri dating hundreds of years before Christ. The universally popular sweet appeared early in the colonies of the Southern United States.

Sugar plums, made from boiled sugar, were eaten in colonial Virginia as well as candy called "marchpane," which was a form of marzipan. In Louisiana, pralines were prepared in New Orleans over two hundred years ago. Inspired by the French version using almonds, the Creoles created their own interpretation by substituting from Louisiana's abundant supply of pecans.

During antebellum times, a confection called "peach leather" was made on hot summer days on South Carolina and Georgia plantations. Pureed peaches were placed in the sun and covered with netting; at night, they were brought inside. After several days of this treatment, the mixture cooked down until it looked like leather.

Candy played an important role in Christmas celebrations on antebellum plantations just as it does today. Trees were decorated with handmade sugarplum baskets and stockings bulged with assorted confections. The laughter of children pulling taffy rang from great house and slaves' quarters alike, for "taffy pulls" were a favorite social activity in both parts of the plantation.

Fudge was unknown until the late 1800s, when students began making it at Eastern girls' schools such as Vassar and Wellesley. Later, fudge making was adopted at Southern female colleges like Wesleyan in Macon, Georgia. There are many Southern variations of traditional chocolate fudge: buttermilk, peanut butter, caramel, and divinity.

Several Southern candies, such as Date Loaf Candy, are based on pecans; others, like Peanut Brittle, rely on peanuts. Florida and Texas grapefruit are spotlighted in Candied Citrus Peel and Kentucky bourbon flavors Walnut Bourbon Balls. Thus, candies become uniquely Southern when spiced from our market basket of local produce.

SHELLEY'S PARTY BALLS

Roll in coconut and chopped nuts

4 ounces cream cheese
2½ cups confectioners' sugar
¾ teaspoon almond extract
¾ teaspoon peppermint
    extract

1 or 2 drops red and green
    food colorings
Grated coconut
Pecans or other nuts, finely
    chopped

Cream cheese and sugar until stiff. Divide dough in half. Flavor one half with almond extract and tint with red food coloring. Flavor the other half with peppermint extract and tint with green food coloring. Chill 2 hours. Roll dough into marble-size balls. Roll pink balls in coconut and green balls in ground nuts. Chill until serving time. Makes 2½ dozen.

OLD–FASHIONED TAFFY

Children love to pull the taffy

2½ cups sugar
½ cup water
¼ cup vinegar
⅛ teaspoon salt

1 tablespoon butter or margarine
1 teaspoon vanilla extract

Combine the sugar, water, vinegar, salt, and butter or margarine in a large, heavy saucepan. Cook, without stirring, over medium heat just until mixture reaches the soft crack stage (270°). Remove from heat. Stir in vanilla. Pour candy onto a well-buttered jelly-roll pan or slab of marble. Let cool to the touch. Butter hands and pull candy until light in color and difficult to pull. Divide candy in half, and pull into a rope, 1 inch in diameter. Cut taffy into 1-inch pieces; wrap each piece individually in wax paper. Makes about 40 pieces.

Molasses was used for making taffy on many Southern plantations instead of sugar. Children would wrap the candy in collard green leaves to separate it and keep it from getting sticky. At times, taffy is still referred to as collard candy.

CANDY AND CONFECTIONS

AUNT ESTHER'S PRALINES
A crisp version of the Creole specialty

1 cup sugar
1 cup boiling water
2 cups sugar
2 cups chopped pecans

1 tablespoon butter or margarine
1 tablespoon vinegar
1 teaspoon vanilla

Caramelize 1 cup sugar. Add boiling water, stirring until all lumps are dissolved. Stir in 2 cups sugar, pecans, butter, and vinegar. Bring to a boil and cook until the syrup forms a soft ball in a cup of water. Remove from stove and stir in vanilla. Continue stirring until mixture starts to glaze over. If it should get too hard, add a few drops of hot water and continue stirring. Drop by the tablespoon onto wax paper. Cool well. Makes 4 to 5 dozen.

LYNDIA'S DIVINITY

No Southern Christmas is complete without it

4 cups sugar
1 cup white karo
1 cup water
Dash salt

4 egg whites
2 teaspoons vanilla
2 cups chopped nuts

Mix sugar, karo, water, and salt. Cook over medium heat until syrup will form a hard ball when dropped in cold water or until a "hard ball" measurement on candy thermometer. While syrup is cooking, beat egg whites with mixer until very stiff. When syrup has reached hard ball stage, remove from heat and pour over stiffly beaten egg whites, very slowly, beating constantly while pouring. When all syrup has been mixed with egg whites and batter is thick, add vanilla and nuts and continue beating with wooden spoon until mixture loses its glaze. Drop by teaspoonsful onto wax paper. (If mixture becomes too hard to drop, place bowl in hot water and continue dipping.) Makes about 36 pieces.

CANDY AND CONFECTIONS

GRANNY'S CARAMEL FUDGE

Jo's mother's recipe

3¼ cups sugar, divided
½ cup butter or margarine
1 cup evaporated milk

1 teaspoon vanilla
1 cup pecans or walnuts

Caramelize ¼ cup sugar in a heavy 3-quart saucepan. Let sugar turn to a light brown. Add butter or margarine, mixing well. Stir in the rest of the sugar and the milk. Cook over medium heat to soft ball stage or 240°, stirring constantly. Remove from heat and add vanilla. Let it cool for about 25 minutes, then beat until thick, smooth, and glossy. Add nuts. Pour into a buttered 9 x 13 inch baking dish. Cut into squares while still warm. Makes about 30 pieces.

Jo's mother makes her caramel icing for cakes by letting it boil to 238°. This amount will ice three layers of the 1-2-3-4 cake. Granny also pours the candy over marshmallows for Caramel-Covered Marshmallows.

EGGNOG FUDGE

Pretty with melted chocolate drizzled over the tops

2 cups sugar
1 cup eggnog, homemade or
  commercial
1 tablespoon light corn syrup
2 tablespoons butter or margarine
1 teaspoon vanilla

$^{1}/_{2}$ cup walnuts or pecans,
  chopped
2 tablespoons semisweet
  chocolate pieces
2 tablespoons butter or margarine

Butter sides of a heavy 3-quart saucepan. Combine sugar, eggnog, and corn syrup. Cook over medium heat stirring constantly, until sugar dissolves and mixture boils. Cook to the soft boil stage (238°), stirring as necessary. Immediately remove from heat and cool to lukewarm (110°) without stirring. Add 2 tablespoons butter and the vanilla. Beat vigorously until it is thick and loses its gloss. Quickly stir in the nuts. Spread in a buttered 8 x 4 x 2 inch pan. In a glass measuring cup combine chocolate and remaining butter. Set cup in a pan with 1 inch of hot water. Melt chocolate and drizzle over the top of fudge. Makes 1 pound.

A candy thermometer is invaluable in candy making.

MISS NINA'S CHOCOLATE FUDGE

Smooth, creamy, perfect texture

2$^1/_2$ cups sugar
1 5-ounce can evaporated milk
$^1/_4$ cup cocoa
2 tablespoons light corn syrup

1 teaspoon vanilla
1 tablespoon butter
1 cup pecans, chopped

Bring sugar, milk, cocoa, and corn syrup to a boil over medium heat. Reduce heat to low and cook slowly until it forms a soft ball in cold water or to 234° on the candy thermometer. Add vanilla and butter. Cool for 10 minutes (approximately). Beat until creamy but not too thick. Stir in pecans. Pour into a buttered 1$^1/_2$-quart dish. When firm, cut into squares. Makes 2$^1/_2$ dozen.

MARTHA WASHINGTON CREAMS

A Southern Classic

2 pounds (2 boxes) confectioners' sugar

1 8-ounce can sweetened condensed milk

1 cup (2 sticks) butter, softened

1 teaspoon vanilla

1 cup pecans, finely chopped

1 16-ounce package semisweet chocolate

A 2- to 3-inch square paraffin, grated

Mix sugar with condensed milk and butter. Add vanilla and pecans. Roll into small balls about $^3/_4$-inch in diameter and place on wax paper. Refrigerate covered until ready to dip. Melt chocolate squares in the top of a double boiler over hot, not boiling, water. Stir in grated paraffin, testing until you get the desired consistency. Spear balls with toothpicks and dip in the melted chocolate. Allow excess to drip off balls and place them on wax paper. When chocolate is set store in airtight container lined with wax paper. The creams keep, chilled, for up to 2 weeks. Makes 200 balls.

This recipe is from Molly Thompson of Florence, Mississippi. The whole family gathers around to make Martha Washington Creams at Christmas.

CANDY AND CONFECTIONS

CANDIED CITRUS PEEL

So pretty and good, you may never throw away another fruit peel

3 grapefruit, preferably pink
6 oranges with thick skins
6 large limes
6 lemons

3 cups sugar, plus enough to
  roll peel in
4 quarts water

Reserve a plastic bag in the freezer to place peel in as you use the fruit. When peeling the fruit keep in mind that you will be using it for this purpose and section fruit attractively. With a knife, make incisions through the skin of each piece of fruit to separate it into six or eight sections from stem end to bottom of fruit. Separate the skin from fruit and place in bags in refrigerator or freezer. It will keep for 3 days in the refrigerator and 3 months in the freezer. Do not remove the white pith from the peel. Place peel in a large, heavy pot and cover with cold water. Bring to a boil and let boil for 30 seconds. Pour into a colander, rinse under cold water, and rinse the pot. Return the peels to the pot and repeat the procedure. Return the peels to the clean pot again and add 3 cups sugar and 4 quarts water. Bring to a boil and boil gently, uncovered, until the skins are transparent. This will take $1^1/_2$ to 2 hours. Cover a cookie sheet with granulated sugar and roll peels in the sugar until well coated. Let them cool and dry for at least 1 hour. Store in glass jars in the refrigerator.

Fruit peels have decorated Southern desserts for many years. They are not only indispensable for fruitcakes but are often used to decorate the many pudding and poached fruit desserts Southerners are fond of. Chocolate-coated, they make welcome gifts and are often used to decorate the tea tray.

CHOCOLATE COATING FOR CANDIED CITRUS PEEL

Dark chocolate is elegant on one end of the peel

4 ounces semisweet chocolate
2 ounces unsweetened chocolate

1 teaspoon butter
Candied citrus peel

Melt chocolate in the top of a double boiler and stir in the butter. Do not let the chocolate get too hot. Dip half the peel in the chocolate. Remove peel and let the excess chocolate drip off for a few seconds. Place peel onto wax paper. You may store in a jar in the refrigerator. Should coat at least 50 pieces.

CHRISTMAS BERRIES
Pretty candies—similar to marzipan

1 can sweetened condensed milk	1 cup ground blanched almonds
4 3½-oz cans flaked coconut	1 teaspoon almond extract
1 6-oz. package strawberry gelatin	Red food coloring as needed

Combine milk, coconut, and ⅓ cup gelatin. Add almonds, almond extract, and food coloring to tint mixture. Chill until firm enough to handle. Form by ½ tablespoons into strawberry shapes and roll in the remaining gelatin to coat. Place on wax paper lined baking sheets and refrigerate. Makes about 60 berries. These will keep up to 2 weeks in the refrigerator.

STEMS FOR BERRIES

2 cups sifted confectioners' sugar	½ cup heavy cream
	Green food coloring

Combine ingredients and put into a pastry bag with a large open star tip. Pipe stem onto top of berry.

Christmas Berries are served at the annual Victorian Christmas Luncheon at Magnolia Hall in Natchez, Mississippi.

DATE LOAF CANDY

Pack in "goody boxes" for Christmas gifts

3 cups sugar
1 cup milk
$1/4$ teaspoon baking soda

2 cups pitted dates, chopped
1 tablespoon butter
1 cup pecans, chopped $1/2$ teaspoon vanilla

Bring sugar and milk to a boil. Add soda, dates, and butter. Cook to soft ball stage (234° on candy thermometer). Add pecans and vanilla. Cook about 5 more minutes. Remove from heat. Beat until it holds its shape. Soak a dish towel in cold water. Wring dry. Spread the towel on a tray. Spoon the candy mixture onto the center of the cloth in a long line. Roll the cloth around the mixture to form a loaf. Place tray with rolled candy in refrigerator. Chill overnight. Slice into thin slices. Makes 5 dozen.

COOKIES AND SMALL CAKES

The joy of cookie making has been celebrated in America since the Dutch introduced the delicious snacks to their colonies. The word "cookie" came from the Dutch word "koekje," meaning "little cake." German and French settlers made similar sweets, and the three methods gradually blended into the repertoire of Southern cuisine.

Although the English preferred the word "biscuit" to "cookie," they brought recipes for small cakes with them to Virginia. Martha Washington is known to have served Shrewsberry Cakes and Jumbles, a buttery cookie that was twisted into various shapes, during Christmas holidays at Mount Vernon.

Seasonings like ginger and many extracts were available in the colonies together with almonds and fruit. Molasses was the sweetener of necessity because sugar was expensive. Molds of different shapes and tin cookie cutters were used to make decorative designs.

Recipes arrived from many sources. Thomas Jefferson, the indefatigable Southern gourmet, discovered French macaroons and meringues in Paris while serving as minister to France and brought them home to Monticello. While president, Jefferson often requested a plateful of cookies with a decanter of wine for a late-night snack.

As always, Southerners were resourceful at using native products. Pecans were often featured in recipes and eventually peanuts came into vogue, notably in famous Peanut Butter Cookies. Southern peanuts and pecans are now America's favorite nuts.

Cookies are more popular than ever in today's South. Bake sales to raise money for charity are widely held and homemade cookies make excellent fund raisers. Cookies appear on almost any party table where the Southern sweet tooth is evident in pick-up desserts as well as savory hors d'oeuvres. Add the endless variety of recipes in regional cookbooks and it becomes obvious that Southern cookie making is still a joy.

RIBBON COOKIES

A really pretty cookie that is nice for special occasions

1 cup margarine
1¼ cups sugar
1 egg, beaten
1 teaspoon vanilla
2½ cups flour
1½ teaspoons baking powder
½ teaspoon salt

¼ cup candied cherries, cut in small pieces
1 square unsweetened chocolate
¼ cup pecans
2 tablespoons poppy seed

Cream margarine and sugar; add egg and vanilla. Sift flour, baking powder, and salt. Add to creamed mixture. Mix well. Divide in three parts. Add cherries to one part, chocolate and pecans to another, poppy seed to the third part. Line a 12 x 4 inch pan with wax paper. Place dough with cherries on bottom, then the chocolate dough and nut mixture, and then the poppy seed mixture. Cover with wax paper. Chill in the refrigerator overnight. Cut loaf in half lengthwise. Slice thin cookies with a sharp knife. Bake on an ungreased cookie sheet in a 375° oven for 10 to 12 minutes. Makes 6 dozen.

SANDIES

Pretty and festive on a party tray

1¹/₂ sticks butter
4 tablespoons confectioners' sugar
2 teaspoons cold water
1 teaspoon vanilla

2 cups flour
¹/₈ teaspoon salt
1 cup pecans, finely chopped
1 cup confectioners' sugar

Cream butter and sugar. Mix in water and vanilla. Add flour slowly, beating well after each addition. Mix in salt. Stir in pecans. Form balls approximately 1 inch in diameter with hands. Bake on greased cookie sheet at 275° for about 40 minutes. When done, roll in confectioners' sugar. Makes 3 dozen.

DELTA MELTING MOMENTS

A melt-in-your-mouth cookie from the Mississippi Delta

$^1/_2$ pound butter
5$^1/_2$ tablespoons confection-
    ers' sugar
1$^1/_4$ cup flour

$^1/_2$ cup cornstarch
$^1/_4$ teaspoon almond extract
$^1/_4$ teaspoon orange extract

Cream butter and sugar. Sift in flour and cornstarch. Mix together. Add flavorings and chill overnight. Shape into balls the size of walnuts and place on a greased cookie sheet. (Do not use butter on the cookie sheet; it will burn.) Flatten the balls with bottom of a small wet glass. Bake at 350° for 10 minutes. Cookies do not brown. Makes 2 dozen.

HEBREW COOKIES
A century-old family secret

1 pound butter or margarine
1¼ cups sugar
3 eggs
3 cups pecans or walnuts

1 cup bourbon
8 to 8½ cups flour
2 cups confectioners' sugar
4 tablespoons cinnamon

Cream the butter and sugar until light. Add the eggs, nuts, and bourbon. Stir in enough flour for a medium-textured dough to roll like a pie crust. Chill the dough for 4 hours or overnight in the refrigerator. Place on a floured board and roll out as for pie dough ⅛ to ¼ inch thick. Cut into ¾ x 2 inch strips. Bake in a preheated 400° oven for 10 to 15 minutes or until firm to the touch. Mix confectioners' sugar and cinnamon together. Roll cookies, while still hot, in the sugar-cinnamon mixture. Makes well over 100 cookies. Store in tins.

Over eighty years ago Mrs. Perkins and Mrs. Henshaw of Jackson, Mississippi, had an aunt who hand stitched beautifully. A neighbor asked her to make a baby bonnet for a new family arrival. The aunt told her that she would not take any amount of money for the bonnet and would only make it if the neighbor would give her the recipe for Hebrew Cookies, a treasured family secret. Now it is a treasured recipe in Mrs. Perkins' and Mrs. Henshaw's family though there is some disagreement on how it should be made. One sister likes her Hebrew Cookies one-eighth of an inch thick while the other likes hers one-fourth of an inch thick. Either way, they both agree that they are the best cookies that they have encountered in their eighty-odd years. Neither sister remembers why the cookies were named Hebrew Cookies.

AUNT PITTYPAT'S JUMBLES

A favorite since Martha Washington's time

1¼ cups sugar
¾ cup margarine
3 eggs
4½ cups flour
3 teaspoons baking powder

½ teaspoon mace
⅔ teaspoon salt
3½ tablespoons orange juice
2 tablespoons lemon juice
1 cup pecans or walnuts, chopped

Cream the sugar and margarine. Add the well-beaten eggs one at a time, then add flour, baking powder, mace, and salt sifted together, alternately with the orange and lemon juice. Taste for seasoning and add more juice if necessary. Stir in the chopped nuts. Chill dough several hours or overnight. Turn onto a slightly floured board and roll ¼ inch. Cut into jumbles with a 2-inch doughnut cutter. Pull them slightly to make more oblong than round. Place on a greased baking sheet, leaving a little space between them, about ½ inch. Bake in a 350° preheated oven for 12 to 15 minutes or until firm to the touch. Makes about 4 dozen. For variety divide the dough into three portions. Mix ingredients as directed, then finish in one of the following ways:

EGG WASH

1 egg yolk

½ cup evaporated milk or sweet cream

Beat the yolk of egg, add the milk or cream to it, and brush over the surface of cookies, applying it with a soft pastry brush. Mixture will keep in the refrigerator for a week. Makes a little over ½ cup.

Brush tops of cut cookies with egg wash and sprinkle with granulated sugar, then bake.

Brush tops of cut cookies with egg wash and place

COOKIES AND SMALL CAKES

chopped or split almonds on each jumble, then bake.
Add ¹/₂ cup seedless raisins to mixture before rolling and
cutting.

PECAN CRISPS

Rich and crunchy—a pecan-lover's dream

1 cup margarine	1/8 teaspoon salt
2 1/2 cups brown sugar	1/2 teaspoon soda
2 eggs, beaten	1 cup pecans, chopped
2 1/2 cups flour	1 teaspoon vanilla

Cream margarine and sugar. Beat in eggs. Sift together flour, salt, and soda. Blend gradually into creamed ingredients. Stir in nuts and vanilla. Drop by teaspoonsful on greased cookie sheet and bake at 350° for approximately 15 minutes. Makes 10 dozen.

GEORGIA PEANUT COOKIES
A yummy drop cookie

$^1/_2$ cup margarine	2 teaspoons baking powder
1 cup sugar	$^1/_2$ teaspoon salt
2 eggs	$^1/_4$ cup milk
2 cups sifted flour	$1^1/_2$ cups chopped peanuts

Cream together margarine and sugar. Add beaten eggs and blend thoroughly. Sift flour, measure, add baking powder and salt, and sift again. Add alternately with milk to creamed mixture. Add nuts and mix only enough to blend. Drop by teaspoonsful onto greased baking sheet. Bake in 400° oven about 10 minutes. Makes 8 dozen $1^1/_2$ inch cookies.

Always preheat the oven and use only one rack. Pans should be at least 2 inches from oven walls. If using two smaller pans, see that they are spaced evenly from each other.

BELL-RINGER MOLASSES COOKIES

Serve with mild cheddar cheese at your next cocktail party

2 cups brown sugar
1 cup shortening
1 egg
1 cup molasses
4 cups all-purpose flour
$^{1}/_{2}$ teaspoon salt

2 teaspoons baking soda
1 teaspoon cinnamon
$^{1}/_{2}$ teaspoon cloves
1 teaspoon vanilla
1 teaspoon lemon extract

Cream sugar, shortening, egg, and molasses (buy dark Jamaican molasses for best flavor). Sift together dry ingredients and gradually add to the creamed mixture. Add vanilla and lemon extract. Chill dough. Form 1-inch balls and place on greased cookie sheet. Bake at 350° for about 12 minutes. May be sprinkled with sugar as soon as removed from oven. Cool cookies slightly before handling. Makes 5 to 6 dozen.

These cookies are sold every fall at the Oktoc Country Store during a fund-raising celebration in Oktoc, Mississippi. They taste even better with cool apple cider.

SIX–FLAVOR REFRIGERATOR COOKIES

Makes one roll each of plain, chocolate, coconut, fruit, nut, and spice

6 cups flour, sifted
4 teaspoons baking powder
$1/2$ teaspoon salt
$1^1/2$ cups margarine
3 cups brown sugar
2 eggs, well beaten
2 teaspoons vanilla
2 squares (2 ounces) chocolate

$1/3$ cup shredded coconut
$1/3$ cups currants, raisins, or chopped dried fruit (dates, apricots, prunes, or figs)
$1/3$ cup nuts, finely chopped (almonds, pecans, peanuts, or walnuts)
$1/2$ teaspoon cinnamon
$1/2$ teaspoon nutmeg

Sift flour, baking powder, and salt. Cream margarine and sugar until fluffy. Add eggs and vanilla. Slowly and gently work flour mixture into creamed mixture. Divide into six equal portions. Leave one portion plain and make variations of remaining dough. Shape into rolls and chill overnight. When firm slice very thin and bake in a 375° oven for 10 to 12 minutes. Makes 10 dozen cookies.

Chocolate: Add 2 ounces melted chocolate to one portion of dough and roll.

Coconut: Add $1/3$ cup shredded coconut to one portion of dough.

Fruit: Add $1/3$ cup of your chosen fruit (soften figs by steaming or boiling in water) to one portion of dough.

Nut: Add $1/3$ cup finely chopped almonds, pecans, peanuts, or walnuts to one portion.

Spice: Add $1/2$ teaspoon cinnamon and $1/2$ teaspoon nutmeg to one portion of dough.

LITTLE LEAGUE OATMEAL COOKIES

Also a winner with the little Miss Teaset crowd when iced and sprinkled with coconut

1½ cups sifted flour
1 cup sugar
½ teaspoon baking soda
1 teaspoon salt
½ teaspoon nutmeg
¾ teaspoon cinnamon
¾ cup margarine
1 egg, well beaten

1 cup mashed ripe banana (2 to 3 bananas)
1¾ cups rolled oats, uncooked
½ cup chopped pecans or walnuts
½ cup raisins
1 cup chocolate chips

Sift into mixing bowl flour, sugar, soda, salt, nutmeg, and cinnamon. Cut in margarine. Add egg, bananas, rolled oats, nuts, raisins, and chocolate chips. Beat until thoroughly blended with a spoon. Drop by teaspoonsful, about 1½ inches apart, onto ungreased cookie sheet. Bake in a 400° oven about 15 minutes, or until edges are browned. Remove from pan immediately and cool on a rack. Makes about 3½ dozen cookies.

BANANA ICING

¾ cup mashed ripe banana
½ teaspoon lemon juice
⅛ teaspoon salt
2 tablespoons softened butter or margarine

2½ cups sifted confectioners' sugar
1 cup grated coconut

Mix the mashed banana with the lemon juice and dash of salt. Cream in the softened butter or margarine. Gradually beat in the confectioners' sugar. Beat until fluffy. Ice the cookies and sprinkle with tinted coconut. To tint coconut, shake white coconut in a covered jar or plastic bag with a few drops of vegetable coloring until tinted. Pink and green are especially nice.

PECAN SOUFFLE TASSIES

Perfect for any party, they make their own crust

1 cup sugar
4 eggs
2 cups milk
$^1/_2$ cup melted margarine
$^1/_2$ cup flour

1 teaspoon vanilla
1 cup pecans, chopped
72 small pecan halves for
   garnish

Place sugar, eggs, milk, margarine, flour, vanilla, and 1 cup chopped pecans in a blender. If blender will not contain the entire mixture, reserve some of the milk to add later. Pour mixture into greased miniature muffin pans, about half full. Place a pecan half on top of each pie. Bake in a preheated 300° oven for 30 to 35 minutes or until a knife in the center comes out clean. Makes about 72 tassies.

To soften hard, dry cookies, put them with a piece of bread into a tightly closed container. Replace the bread every few days, for it molds easily.

COOKIES AND SMALL CAKES

MAIDS OF HONOR

An English teatime favorite adopted by the South

$^3/_4$ cup butter or margarine, softened	2 cups flour
$^1/_2$ cup sugar	$^1/_4$ teaspoon salt

Preheat oven to 350°. Grease bottoms and sides of $3^1/_2$ dozen miniature muffin tins. Cream butter or margarine with sugar and gradually mix in flour and salt. Pinch off small pieces of dough and press into tins, forming a cup. Set aside.

FILLING

2 eggs	$^1/_2$ cup almond paste
$^1/_2$ cup sugar	$1^1/_2$ tablespoons sherry
2 tablespoons flour	$^1/_3$ teaspoon nutmeg
2 tablespoons butter, melted	Raspberry or strawberry preserves

Beat eggs well and add sugar and flour slowly. Mix in butter, almond paste, sherry, and nutmeg. Spoon $^1/_2$ teaspoon of preserves into each muffin cup. (Be careful not to put in too much.) Fill muffin cups with custard. Bake at 350° for approximately 30 minutes. Makes $3^1/_2$ dozen.

These delicious tarts were brought to the mid-Atlantic South by English settlers, and became quite popular. Some claim the very old sweet was named for the maids of honor at the court of Elizabeth 1. Other sources report they were first baked by Anne Boleyn for the court of Henry VIII when she was maid of honor to Catherine of Aragon. Whether they helped Anne lure Henry from Catherine is open to debate.

COCONUT MACAROONS

From the Cloister Hotel at Sea Island, Georgia

5 ounces almond paste

20 ounces ($2^1/_2$ cups) granulated sugar

1 cup (about 8) egg whites

1 teaspoon vanilla extract

10 ounces coconut, shredded

$1^1/_2$ ounces (3 tablespoons)
  all-purpose flour

Break up almond paste into small pieces. Add sugar a little at a time, using a mixer or hands, until completely mixed and looks like coarse meal. Gradually add the egg whites, scraping down the bowl at least once. Add vanilla. Place bowl in a hot water bath (to heat), stirring the mixture constantly. Heat until the mixture is too hot to touch. Set aside. Blend coconut and flour. Then mix all ingredients together using a wooden spatula. Drop by teaspoonsful or fill a pastry bag with the mixture and drop through a number 8 star tube onto a paper pan liner or brown paper that has been cut to fit your cookie sheet. Bake in a preheated 350° oven until golden brown, about 15 to 20 minutes. Let the macaroons cool completely before removing them. Let them dry a little on racks. Store in airtight tins. Makes about 4 dozen.

Note: The coconut might be dry at times and therefore will absorb more moisture, causing the mixture to be too stiff and hard to pipe out. This can be corrected by adding a little more egg white to the mixture. Pat Ross, a noted cooking instructor, advises that if dough is not stiff enough you may add ground almonds to the dough to stiffen it. This also gives it an interesting crunch.

BINNY'S BEIGNETS
New Orleans French Market doughnuts

1 package yeast	2 tablespoons corn oil
$^1/_4$ cup warm water	4-5 cups flour
$^1/_3$ cup sugar	2 eggs beaten
1 cup warm milk	Oil for frying
$^1/_2$ teaspoon salt	Confectioners' sugar

Dissolve yeast in warm water. Add sugar; mix in warm milk, salt, corn oil, and part of flour. Mix well. Alternately add eggs and enough flour to make a soft, non-sticky dough. Knead well and place in a covered, greased bowl for 30 minutes. Divide dough in half. Keep unused part of dough covered. Roll out to $^1/_4$ inch thickness and cut into rectangles 2 x 3 inches. At this point you may refrigerate overnight or freeze a few weeks. Cook only 3 or 4 at a time in deep fat heated to 360°, turning often. Drain well and serve with confectioners' sugar. Makes 3 to 4 dozen.

CREOLE LACE COOKIES

Pecan lace cookies from Lee Barnes Cooking School in New Orleans

1¹/₃ cups pecans, chopped
1 cup sugar
4 tablespoons flour
¹/₃ teaspoon baking powder

¹/₈ teaspoon salt
¹/₂ cup (1 stick) butter, melted
2 teaspoons vanilla
1 egg, beaten

Mix well the pecans, sugar, flour, baking powder, and salt. Add the melted butter, vanilla, and egg. Drop onto foil-lined cookie sheet in scant teaspoonsful. Place about 3 inches apart. Bake in a 325° oven for 8 to 12 minutes, depending upon your oven. Let cool. Peel off the foil. Makes about 4 dozen.

CORRINE'S SOUTHERN BELLE BROWNIES

Iced brownies that are perfect for parties or bake sales

1 cup butter or margarine	2 cups flour
$^1/_2$ cup cocoa	$^1/_2$ teaspoon baking powder
2 cups sugar	$^1/_4$ teaspoon salt
4 eggs	3 teaspoons vanilla

Melt $^1/_2$ cup butter or margarine with cocoa in the top of a double boiler. Set aside to cool. Cream the other $^1/_2$ cup butter or margarine with sugar. Add the cocoa mixture. Add eggs and beat well. Sift flour, baking powder, and salt together. Add to the above mixture a little at a time. Stir in vanilla. Pour batter into a greased 11 x 12 inch or 10 x 15 inch pan. Bake in a 325° oven for 35 minutes. When cool frost with One-Minute Fudge Frosting. Makes about 24 brownies.

ONE–MINUTE FUDGE FROSTING

$^1/_4$ cup butter or margarine	1 cup sugar
$^1/_4$ cup cocoa	2 teaspoons vanilla
$^1/_4$ cup milk	$^1/_2$ cup pecans

Melt butter or margarine and cocoa. Add milk and sugar. Bring to a rolling boil. Boil for 1 minute. Remove from heat, add vanilla. Beat while hot until it begins to thicken. Add nuts and spread on brownies. If any icing is left drop on wax paper and place a pecan on the top. It makes great candy.

LIZZIES
Fruit and nuts look like jewels in a miniature cake confection

1 cup butter, room temperature
1 cup brown sugar
4 eggs
3 cups flour
1 teaspoon nutmeg
1 teaspoon cinnamon
$^1/_4$ teaspoon ground cloves
4 cups pecans (3 cups chopped, 1 cup halves)

1 cup candied cherries, chopped into fourths
$^1/_2$ cup citron
1 8-ounce box pitted dates, chopped
1 cup candied pineapple, cut into small wedges
3 tablespoons milk
$^1/_2$ cup blackberry wine or orange juice ($^1/_3$ cup bourbon may be substituted)

Cream butter and sugar well. Add eggs one at a time, beating well after each addition. Add $^1/_2$ cup flour and mix well. Add spices. In a separate bowl place nuts (both pieces and halves) and cut-up fruit and add $^1/_2$ cup flour, stirring to coat all of the pieces well. Fold fruit mixture into creamed mixture. Add milk, wine, orange juice or bourbon, and balance of flour. Mix batter well. Drop by teaspoonsful onto foil-lined cookie sheet or into tiny paper cups for miniature cakes. Bake for 20 minutes at 350° or until light brown (they will still be soft). Makes about 10 dozen.

It is unknown where Lizzies got their name. They have been a popular fruitcake cookie for as long as anybody can remember.

Sprinkle small squares of fruitcake with sherry or bourbon. Coat with confectioners' sugar. Nice for parties or to serve with tea.

OVERNIGHT SLICED FRUIT COOKIES

A delicious cookie recipe from the past

3/4 cup butter

2 cups light brown sugar

3 eggs

1 teaspoon baking soda

1 tablespoon water

1/4 cup finely chopped citron

1/4 cup finely chopped raisins

3/4 cup pecans, finely chopped

1/4 teaspoon almond extract

3 1/2 cups flour

Sugar

Put butter in a mixing bowl and set the bowl over hot water until the butter softens; remove the bowl, add brown sugar and eggs, and beat until the mixture is blended. Dissolve soda in the tablespoon water. Add to the butter-sugar mixture. Add fruits, nuts, and almond extract and stir in the flour. Turn into a greased bread pan. Set the pan in the refrigerator overnight or longer. When ready to bake the cookies, turn the dough onto a bread board and cut into very thin slices. Place on a greased baking sheet, sprinkle with sugar, and bake in a hot oven at 425° for 12 to 15 minutes. Leave plenty of room between the cookies as they spread. Makes about 3 1/2 dozen. If smaller cookies are desired, the cookie dough may be placed in small bread pans or rolled in wax paper and refrigerated. This recipe makes the large, old-fashioned kind.

CUSTARDS, PUDDINGS, AND MOLDS

Southerners who settled along the Atlantic coast were as passionate about puddings as their English ancestors. During the early 1700s, plum and other fruit puddings were the desserts of choice. Later in the century, many colonists prospered; soon hardscrabble farms expanded into lush plantations, resulting in an abundance of farm-fresh eggs, heavy cream, and homegrown fruit and nuts. Plantation wives used these riches to make creamy English desserts: trifle, tipsy parson, baked and boiled custard.

Southerners may have inherited their love for puddings from the English, but the French also left their mark. When Thomas Jefferson returned from serving as minister to France, he brought home a wealth of recipes for French puddings and molds: Charlotte Russe, floating island, and wine jelly. These unfamiliar dishes were welcomed enthusiastically by early Virginia hostesses who were fond of serving a lavish assortment of pretty desserts. Mousses and charlottes could be made as fancy as one pleased with the popular fluted metal molds. Shimmering, jewel-toned jellies, supported by the addition of gelatinous boiled calves' feet, also made spectacular displays.

Sumptuous creams and molds were relished by the genteel society of Charleston. Surprisingly, they held up well in the city's notoriously humid weather. Charlestonians had disdain for one pudding, however; they disliked the idea of eating sweetened rice and would have nothing to do with rice pudding. Elsewhere in the South, the average citizen preferred rice, fruit, or bread pudding to creamy custard.

Today we regard charlottes, trifles, and plum pudding as celebration desserts—reserved for holidays and special occasions. Simpler fare like banana pudding, floating island, and kiss custard are comfort foods whose soothing taste fills us with nostalgia. Together with other refrigerator desserts they will remain popular for a long time.

APPLE CHARLOTTE WITH BRANDY SAUCE

Joe Middleton's interpretation of this classic dessert

8 to 10 slices firm-textured
   white bread, trimmed of
   crusts, buttered on one side
8 green tart apples
4 tablespoons butter

$^{1}/_{4}$ cup sugar
Grated rind of 1 lemon
1 teaspoon cinnamon
1 teaspoon ground ginger
$^{1}/_{2}$ teaspoon ground cloves
3 ounces applejack or Calvados

Preheat oven to 400°. Line the bottom and sides of a $1^{1}/_{2}$ - quart charlotte mold or casserole with the bread slices, buttered side to the mold. Peel, core, and slice the apples. Melt the butter in a large skillet. Add the sliced apples, sugar, grated lemon rind, cinnamon, ginger, cloves, and applejack. Fry slowly until the apples are slightly softened. Pour the apples into the mold, allowing the excess to form a mound around the rim. Bake for 20 minutes, then cover with aluminum foil and continue cooking for another 20 minutes or until the apples are completely cooked and the edges of the bread have browned slightly. Cool for at least 1 hour before unmolding and serve with brandy sauce. Serves 6.

BRANDY SAUCE

$^{1}/_{2}$ cup apricot glaze (if not
   available see note)
1 ounce brandy
1 cup apple juice

Juice of 1 lemon
$^{1}/_{8}$ teaspoon ground ginger
1 teaspoon cornstarch

Combine apricot glaze, brandy, $^{3}/_{4}$ cup apple juice, lemon juice, and ginger in a saucepan and bring to a boil. Add cornstarch to the remaining $^{1}/_{4}$ cup apple juice to dissolve. Return to a boil. Remove from heat and serve warm.

Note: To make an apricot glaze, heat $^1/_2$ cup apricot jam or preserves with 1 teaspoon water until it melts, then put through a strainer to remove any lumps.

Joe Middleton is one of the South's favorite chefs, caterers, and cooking school teachers. He has been chef at the Hyatt Regency in Houston; the Routh Street Café, Dallas; the Waldorf Astoria in New York; and Commander's Palace in New Orleans. He has taught cooking in Lee Barnes Cooking School in New Orleans, Anna Muffaleto's Cordon Bleu Cooking School in New York, and has taught culinary arts at Tulane University in New Orleans.

Almost any bowl that splays out at the sides can be used for a pudding mold. For straight-sided desserts use a springform mold.

RICE PUDDING

A tasty top-of-the-stove method that you make ahead

¹/₂ cup long grain white rice	¹/₂ cup sugar
1 cup water	2 teaspoons vanilla
4¹/₄ cups milk	¹/₈ teaspoon salt
¹/₄ cup white raisins	1 teaspoon cinnamon
3 egg yolks	¹/₂ teaspoon nutmeg

Combine rice and water in a 2-quart saucepan. Bring to boil and boil 8 to 10 minutes or until water is absorbed. Stir in milk and return to boiling. Lower heat and simmer, stirring often, for 25 minutes. Add raisins and cook 5 to 10 minutes longer or until rice is tender. Beat yolks in a small bowl until frothy. Whisk in sugar, vanilla, and salt. Stir ¹/₃ cup hot rice mixture into yolks and return mixture to saucepan. Cook over very low heat for 2 minutes or until slightly thickened. Mixture should be loose and creamy. Pour into 1¹/₂-quart casserole dish; cover surface of pudding with plastic wrap (place plastic wrap on rice surface). Refrigerate overnight. When ready to serve, remove plastic wrap and sprinkle with cinnamon and nutmeg. Bake in a preheated 425° oven for about 5 minutes or until crusty on top. Serves 8.

SWEET POTATO PUDDING

Not too sweet, with a delicate flavor

2 cups sweet potatoes, mashed	1 egg
2 tablespoons sugar	$^{1}/_{3}$ cup milk
1 teaspoon allspice	$^{1}/_{4}$ cup melted butter
$^{1}/_{2}$ teaspoon salt	$^{1}/_{4}$ cup grated coconut
	$^{1}/_{4}$ cup raisins

Mash sweet potatoes with a mixer until smooth. Add sugar, allspice, and salt. Beat egg and mix with milk; add to potato mixture. Stir in melted butter, coconut, and raisins. Place mixture in a pie plate and bake in a preheated 375° oven for 20 minutes, or until heated through. Serve warm, with whipped cream or ice cream. Serves 4.

This recipe is from the Mount Calvary Missionary Baptist Church, Tougaloo, Mississippi. It was contributed by Mrs. Katie Rhone.

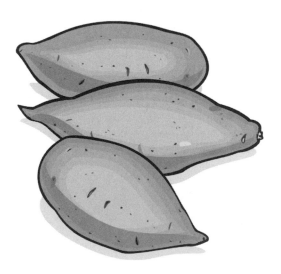

BINNY WEBB'S BREAD PUDDING

An elegant version of a cozy dish

$^1/_2$ cup dried apricots,
   chopped with scissors
$^1/_2$ cup seedless dark raisins
2 cups water, boiling
$^1/_4$ cup Kirsch
1 quart milk
4 egg yolks
1 cup sugar

1 teaspoon vanilla
1 cup heavy cream
10 slices French bread, cut $^1/_4$
   inch thick
3 tablespoons unsalted butter,
   softened
2 tablespoons confectioners'
   sugar

Preheat oven 325°. Place apricots and raisins in a bowl and pour boiling water over them. Let stand five minutes and drain. Mix fruit with Kirsch. Place a large pan partially filled with water in oven. Bring milk to a boil. Mix eggs, egg yolks, sugar, and vanilla together with a wire whisk. Add cream to the milk and mix well. Gradually add this to the egg mixture. Strain through a fine sieve. Butter a 2-quart rectangular or oval baking dish. Place fruit in bottom. Butter bread and place, buttered side up, on top of the fruit. Pour milk mixture through strainer over bread. Place baking dish in the bottom third of the oven in pan of water. The water should cover half the dish. Bake 45 to 60 minutes or until a knife inserted in the middle of the pudding comes out clean. Sprinkle confectioners' sugar on top and glaze under the broiler, watching carefully that it doesn't burn. Serve at room temperature with Cognac Sauce. Serves 6 to 8.

COGNAC SAUCE

3 egg yolks
1 cup sugar
1 teaspoon vanilla
$1^1/_2$ cups milk

1 tablespoon cornstarch
3 tablespoons water
1 ounce cognac

Beat yolks and add sugar and vanilla. Heat milk to the boiling point and gradually add to the eggs. Cook over low heat until mixture is very hot. Combine water and cornstarch and add to the mixture. Stir until sauce coats a spoon. Remove from heat and stir in brandy. This sauce can also be used over fruit or pound cake.

In the early days bread pudding was known as a poor man's dessert. The creativity of frugal Southern cooks was challenged by having to decide how to make a dessert out of leftover bread, milk, eggs, and butter. Resourceful housewives used dried or fresh fruit and whatever spirits they had on hand for flavoring. Creole cooks raised bread pudding to a loftier position with recipes like this.

Add lemon juice and crushed mint leaves to taste to apricot preserves for a delicious cake, bread pudding, or ice cream topping.

BREAD PUDDING WITH RUM SAUCE

The ultimate comfort food

6 slices day old bread
1 teaspoon cinnamon
$^1/_2$ cup seedless raisins
2 tablespoons butter, melted
4 eggs

$^1/_2$ cup plus 2 tablespoons sugar
2 cups milk
1 teaspoon vanilla

Break bread into small pieces in a baking dish. Sprinkle cinnamon over bread and add raisins and melted butter. Toast bread mixture lightly in oven set at 350°. Mix eggs, sugar, milk, and vanilla and pour over bread mixture. Bake for about 30 minutes at 350° or until solid. Serves about 8.

RUM SAUCE

2 cups milk
$^1/_2$ stick butter
$^1/_2$ cup sugar
2 tablespoons flour

1 tablespoon cooking oil
1 teaspoon nutmeg
1 teaspoon vanilla
3 tablespoons rum, or to taste

Place milk, butter, and sugar in saucepan. Let come to boil. Thicken with roux made of flour and oil. Remove from heat. Add nutmeg, vanilla, and rum. Serve over pudding.

This recipe is from Mary Mahoney's Old French House Restaurant, located in a beautiful two-hundred-year-old house on the Mississippi Gulf Coast.

NANIE'S PLUM PUDDING

Make it your Christmas specialty

1^1/$_2$ cups sugar

4 eggs

3 cups raisins

2 cups flour, sifted

1^1/$_2$ cups margarine or butter, cold

1^1/$_2$ cups bread crumbs

^{1}/$_3$ cup milk

^{1}/$_2$ cup citron (optional)

1 rounded teaspoon baking
  powder

1 teaspoon nutmeg

1 teaspoon ground cloves

1 teaspoon cinnamon

^{1}/$_2$ tablespoon orange mar-
  malade

Cream sugar and eggs, one egg at a time. Add raisins that have been coated with flour. Slice cold butter and add to mixture, then add other ingredients. Put aside about 1 cup of the plum pudding mixture for the sauce. Cook in plum pudding steamer for 3 hours. Check water level every hour.

SAUCE

1 cup plum pudding mixture

5 cups water

1 cup sugar

Rind of 1 or 2 oranges,
  cut in small pieces

Cook until thickened. Spoon over pudding. Serves 12 to 14.

From Vintage Vicksburg, *compiled by the Junior Auxiliary of historic Vicksburg, Mississippi.*

If lady fingers are used to line a mold, split and place the curved sides against the form. To make an even top, slice each section to a point by cutting it diagonally and placing it with the pointed end toward the middle. You may also cut a small round for the center.

CABINET PUDDING

Macaroons and cream compose a celebration dessert

2 tablespoons gelatin
1 cup cold water
6 eggs, separated
8 tablespoons sugar
$^1/_2$ cup sherry
$^1/_2$ teaspoon almond extract
$1^1/_2$ dozen macaroons,
    crumbled

1 cup pecans, chopped
1 10-ounce jar maraschino
    cherries, sliced
1 cup heavy cream, whipped
4 tablespoons sugar
$^1/_2$ teaspoon vanilla

Soak gelatin in cold water, then heat until dissolved. Beat egg yolks, add sugar, slowly, and continue beating until creamy. Add sherry. Cook mixture in top of a double boiler over medium heat until thick. Cool. Meanwhile, beat egg whites until stiff. Combine whites, egg yolk mixture, and gelatin slowly on low speed of mixer. Add almond extract. Pour one-third of custard into a $1^1/_2$ -quart mold. Add layer of macaroon crumbs, chopped pecans, and sliced cherries. Alternate layers until there are 3 layers of each mixture; leave out $^1/_4$ cup macaroon crumbs. Whip cream; sweeten with sugar; flavor with vanilla; spread over pudding. Top with remaining crumbs. Refrigerate until serving time. Serves 12.

Add 1 tablespoon of any liqueur to $^1/_2$ pint of heavy cream whipped with $^1/_4$ cup confectioners' sugar to develop your own "spécialité de la maison".

FRANCES'S ANGEL BAVARIAN CREAM

A beauty from Mary Leigh's Virginia cousin

2 cups milk
4 eggs, separated
1 cup sugar
2 tablespoons flour
$^1/_8$ teaspoon salt
1 tablespoon gelatin
$^1/_4$ cup cold water

1$^1/_2$ teaspoons vanilla
1 cup heavy cream, whipped
1 Angel Food Cake
$^1/_2$ pint heavy cream,
   whipped
4 tablespoons sugar
1$^1/_2$ teaspoons vanilla

Scald milk in top of a double boiler. Meanwhile, beat egg
yolks. Gradually add sugar, flour, and salt, beating until
thick. Add a little milk to egg mixture, beating constantly.
Transfer egg mixture to milk on the stove and cook until it
thickens. While hot, stir in gelatin that has been soaked in
cold water. Cool. Add 1$^1/_2$ teaspoons vanilla. Beat egg whites
until stiff. Fold into yolk mixture. Whip 1 cup heavy cream
and combine with custard. Slice thin layers from top and
bottom of angel food cake. Break the middle section into
small chunks. Place top slice in bottom of an angel food cake
pan. Pour in a layer of custard, then add a layer of cake
chunks. Continue alternating custard and cake, ending with
the slice of cake cut from the bottom. Refrigerate overnight.
Unmold. Whip cream and flavor with 4 tablespoons sugar
and 1$^1/_2$ teaspoons vanilla. Ice cake. Refrigerate several hours
until time to serve. Cut into slices. Top with strawberry
sauce. Serves 10.

STRAWBERRY SAUCE

2 cups strawberries, sliced   2 tablespoons cornstarch
$^2/_3$ cup sugar   2 tablespoons cassis

Mash berries with a spoon. Add sugar and cornstarch; cook until thick. Stir in cassis. Cool. Chill until serving time. Makes 1 pint.

Use a double boiler for top-of-the-stove custards and sauces. Cook over —not in—hot water.

MY MOTHER'S KISS CUSTARD

Mary Leigh's mother's version of floating island

3 eggs, separated	4 cups milk
1 cup sugar	$1/2$ teaspoon vanilla
2 tablespoons flour	$1/2$ teaspoon almond extract
$1/4$ teaspoon salt	1 tablespoon sugar

Beat egg yolks; gradually mix in dry ingredients. Add milk slowly. Cook over low heat until mixture thickens, stirring constantly; will become firmer after chilling. Add vanilla and almond extract. Pour into a 6-cup glass baking dish. Beat egg whites, mixing in 1 tablespoon sugar. Spoon over custard in soft mounds. Place in broiler to brown tips of meringue. Chill. Serves 6.

CREME BRULEE

Impressive but easy—can be made ahead

16 ounces heavy cream
$^3/_4$ cup sugar
8 egg yolks

2 teaspoons vanilla
8 tablespoons brown sugar

Heat the cream in a double boiler over simmering water until hot but not boiling. Stir in sugar and dissolve. Preheat oven to 325°. Beat egg yolks thoroughly. Gently add the hot cream and vanilla. Pour into eight 6- to 8-ounce ramekins and place them in a large pan filled with warm water. Water should come halfway up the side of dishes. Bake for approximately 1 hour and 15 minutes or until a dinner knife inserted around the edges comes out clean. Cool. Cover with plastic wrap and chill until cold. May be made to this point a day in advance. Sprinkle each custard with 1 tablespoon sifted brown sugar. Preheat the broiler. Broil the custards close to the heat for about a minute, watching constantly until sugar is caramelized. When cool, you may serve immediately or return to the refrigerator for several hours until serving time. Serves 8.

CHARLOTTE RUSSE

Sumptuous and elegant; your guests will remember it

1¼ cups milk
2 egg yolks, beaten
½ cup sugar
⅛ teaspoon salt
1¼ tablespoons gelatin
¼ cup cold water
2 egg whites, stiffly beaten

1 cup heavy cream
5 tablespoons confectioners'
   sugar
3½ tablespoons sherry
1 teaspoon vanilla
1 dozen ladyfingers, split

Scald milk in a double boiler over medium heat. Beat egg yolks; add sugar and salt. Remove milk from stove; stir in egg yolk mixture; return to stove and cook until it slightly thickens. Soak gelatin in cold water for 5 minutes. Add to milk mixture and cool. Beat and fold in egg whites. Whip cream and add confectioners' sugar. Fold into custard. Add flavorings. Line a 6-cup mold or serving bowl with split ladyfingers. Pour in custard. Chill until firm. Serve in dessert or sherbet dishes. Serve plain or top with whipped cream. Serves 6.

JOE MIDDLETON'S PRALINE SOUFFLE

A Creole soufflé served with Caramel Sauce

1 cup cream
5 tablespoons flour
$^1/_2$ cup dark brown sugar
4 egg yolks
$^1/_2$ cup roasted pecans,
   ground in processor

6 egg whites
$^1/_8$ teaspoon salt
$^1/_2$ teaspoon cream of tartar
2 tablespoons sugar

Combine cream, flour, and brown sugar in a small saucepan. Bring to a boil while whisking. Cool slightly. Add yolks and pecans. Set aside. In bowl of mixer beat egg whites with salt and cream of tartar. Beat to soft peaks. Slowly add sugar. Beat to stiff peaks. Fold whites into pecan mixture. Place soufflé into 6 chilled and buttered ramekins. Place in 400° oven. Bake for approximately 15 minutes. Serve immediately with Caramel Sauce.

CARAMEL SAUCE

1 cup dark brown sugar
$^1/_4$ cup white sugar

$^1/_2$ cup white corn syrup
1 cup cream

Combine the brown sugar, white sugar, corn syrup, and cream. Bring to a boil. Remove from heat and cool. Serves 6.

BANANA PUDDING

Comfort food for children and adults

12 ounces (or more) vanilla
  wafers
5 or 6 bananas, sliced
3 eggs, separated
1 cup sugar
3 tablespoons flour

Dash of salt
1 12-ounce can evaporated
  milk
1 teaspoon vanilla
2 tablespoons sugar
$^1/_2$ teaspoon cream of tartar

Line bottom and sides of a lightly buttered 2-quart baking dish with vanilla wafers. Place a layer of sliced bananas over wafers. Beat egg yolks with mixer until thick and lemon-colored. Gradually mix in 1 cup sugar, the flour, and the salt. Add milk slowly, beating well. Place mixture in top of a double boiler and cook over simmering water until thick. Remove from heat, add vanilla, and cool. Pour half of mixture over bananas. Layer again with wafers, banana slices, and custard. Beat egg whites until soft peaks form; gradually add 2 tablespoons sugar and cream of tartar. Beat until stiff peaks form; spread over pudding. Bake at 350° for 10 minutes or until golden. May be served warm, but chilling improves flavor. Serves 8.

ANN FOURNET'S CHOCOLATE TERRINE

Chocolate topped with raspberry purée, swimming in custard sauce

3 cups heavy cream
1/2 cup butter
20 ounces semisweet chocolate, melted

4 extra large egg yolks
1 cup almonds, chopped

Heat cream to a simmer; add butter (cut into small pieces) and melt. Add melted chocolate and stir until smooth. Stir in egg yolks, one at a time; add chopped almonds. Pour into a greased 1 1/2-quart mold or springform pan. If using springform pan, be certain to tape seams. Place in large, shallow pan of hot water and bake at 350° for 1 1/2 hours. Cool. Chill. When ready to serve, cut into squares. Spoon 4 tablespoons Crème Anglaise onto individual dessert plates. Place chocolate squares in sauce; top with spoonsful of raspberry purée. Serves 12.

Raspberry purée: Thaw 2 packages raspberries in light syrup. Drain. Blend in blender or processor, then strain. Refrigerate until ready to serve.

CREME ANGLAISE

6 large egg yolks
2/3 cup sugar
4 tablespoons flour

2 cups milk
1 teaspoon vanilla
1 teaspoon almond extract

Mix egg yolks with 1/3 cup sugar and 4 tablespoons flour. Bring milk and remaining sugar to a boil. Add a small amount of milk mixture to yolk mixture. Then add yolk mixture to remaining milk mixture. Cook, stirring constantly over low heat until the mixture thickens. Add extracts. Chill.

WHITE CHOCOLATE COEUR A LA CREME

Garnished with strawberries and raspberry aspic and sauce, it is perfect for a wedding reception

1 cup cottage cheese
1 cup cream cheese, room temperature
$^1/_2$ cup sour cream
6 ounces white chocolate, shaved or chopped into small pieces
$^1/_2$ cup heavy cream, whipped

1 cup confectioners' sugar
$^1/_2$ teaspoon vanilla extract
1 recipe raspberry aspic (recipe below)
1 quart strawberries, whole with stems on
1 recipe raspberry sauce (recipe below)

Line a heart-shaped coeur à la crème mold with cheese-cloth that has been rinsed in cold water. Wring out and place in mold, allowing excess cheesecloth to hang over the edge. Mix cottage cheese, softened cream cheese, and sour cream with an electric mixer. Melt white chocolate by placing in a bowl that has been warmed in hot water. (It may not be all melted, but if it is in small enough pieces, the mixer will finish blending it.) Beat with an electric mixer until blended; add to cream mixture. Whip the heavy cream and fold it into the cheese and chocolate mixture. Add confectioners' sugar and vanilla and spoon into the mold. Fold cheesecloth over the top; cover with plastic wrap. Chill thoroughly. It will keep in the refrigerator for 3 days. It may also be frozen for a week. To serve, open cheesecloth, invert the mold on a plate, and carefully remove the cheesecloth. Serve it with chopped raspberry aspic and lightly sweetened whole fresh strawberries attractively placed around the heart-shaped mold. Spoon raspberry sauce over strawberries and a little on the coeur à la crème, if desired.

RASPBERRY ASPIC

1 tablespoon unflavored gelatin
1/3 cup cold water
2 to 3 tablespoons sugar

1/3 cup framboise (raspberry liqueur)
1 10-ounce package frozen raspberries (to equal 2/3 cup)

Soak gelatin in cold water in a saucepan. Place over low heat and simmer to dissolve. Add sugar, stirring just long enough for it to dissolve. Remove from heat and stir in framboise. Place raspberries in the blender and liquefy. Strain out seeds, measure 2/3 cup, and add to aspic. Pour aspic into a square cake pan, cover, and refrigerate. When ready to serve, turn out on a plate and chop into small squares. Makes a little over 1 cup. Recipe may be doubled, if more aspic is desired.

RASPBERRY SAUCE

1 10-ounce package raspberries, defrosted

1/4 cup sugar
2 tablespoons framboise

Purée raspberries and strain out seeds. Combine with sugar and framboise. Drizzle over the strawberries and the coeur à la crème, if desired. This recipe serves 8. It may be served with thin crisp cookies for a buffet. In this manner it will serve 35.

Jo created this recipe especially for her daughter Emily's wedding reception.

CUSTARDS, PUDDINGS, AND MOLDS

POTS DE CREME
An elegant chocolate mousse made quickly in a blender

6 ounces semisweet chocolate
  bits
$^1/_4$ cup scalded milk
3 tablespoons brewed coffee,
  double strength

2 eggs
2 tablespoons Grand Marnier
$^1/_2$ cup heavy cream, whipped
6 candied violets (optional)

Combine chocolate bits, scalded milk, and hot coffee in blender. Blend for 1 minute. Add eggs and Grand Marnier to the mixture and blend 2 more minutes. Pour mousse into 6 pots de crème; place the tops on them and chill in the refrigerator several hours. The pots de crème may be made several days in advance. To serve, whip the cream and place a teaspoon or two on the pots de crème. Garnish with a candied violet, if desired. The little pots de crème also make an elegant presentation with a small amount of Grand Marnier floating on the top of each without the whipped cream or candied violet. Serves 6.

FRUIT DESSERTS

Fruit has flourished in the mild climate and fertile soil of the South since before the arrival of the earliest settlers. Every season brings its joys: spring berries, summer peaches and melons, fall apples, and winter oranges. With the quantity of rural roadside stands and urban farmers' markets, finding fresh produce at peak flavor is seldom a problem. This bounty from Mother Nature makes fruit desserts popular grand finales in most homes.

Some fruits have thrived in the South since before recorded history. Strawberries grew so thickly in Virginia when European settlers arrived that one Englishman is known to have complained that he could hardly walk without stepping on them. Indians were fond of the heart-shaped berries and held annual strawberry harvest celebrations. Blueberries and blackberries also grow well in Southern soil and their season is awaited with anticipation.

Brought to America by the Spaniards in the 1600s, peaches grow abundantly throughout the lower South and have inspired a host of desserts. Oranges are another Spanish contribution, brought by de Soto and Ponce de Leon. Oranges are used to make ambrosia—considered the quintessential Southern dessert.

Plump, green watermelons, whose seeds were brought from Africa by the slaves, are another popular fruit with Southerners, who like to cool off with a chilled slice on a hot day.

Apples grow best in the cooler climate of Virginia and West Virginia. They are less perishable than most fruits and were dried and stored in cellars for winter pie making during earlier times.

With typical resourcefulness, the first Southerners made do with the foods at hand, creating recipes on the spot for such delicacies as stewed fruit with dumplings, fritters, crisps, and roly-polys. Their legacy became the inspiration for our fruit desserts today.

FRUIT DESSERTS

AMBROSIA

An early marriage of coconut and tropical fruit

8 oranges
3 bananas
8 slices canned pineapple,
   juice reserved

3$^1/_2$ -ounce can angel flake
   coconut
$^2/_3$ cup sugar
$^2/_3$ cup sherry
Maraschino cherries

Peel oranges and remove all white membrane; cut into sections. Slice bananas. Cut pineapple slices into chunks. Place a layer of orange slices in the bottom of a crystal or glass bowl. Spoon a layer of sugar and splash a few spoonsful of sherry over the oranges. Add a layer of bananas, then a layer of sugar and sherry. Next, add a layer of pineapple. Sprinkle with sugar and sherry. Last, add a layer of coconut, topped with sugar and sherry. Repeat process until all ingredients are used. Pour pineapple juice from the can over all. Chill for at least 3 hours. Decorate the top with maraschino cherries and a final sprinkling of coconut. Serves 8 to 10.

ORANGES ALASKA
Divinity Meringue tops an orange shell filled with fruit and ice cream

3 large navel oranges or 6 small
   oranges
1 banana

$^1/_4$ cup sugar
6 rounded tablespoons vanilla
   ice cream

Cut 3 large oranges in half or remove about one-third of the tops from 6 small oranges. Carefully remove pulp, gently scraping out the white pith from shells. Dice pulp, removing seeds and membrane. Mix with diced peeled bananas. (Oranges may be prepared the day before and stored covered in the refrigerator.) Sprinkle fruit with sugar, cover, and let stand in refrigerator for several hours if necessary. When ready to serve, make meringue. Place 1 rounded tablespoon vanilla ice cream in each shell. Fill with fruit and cover with meringue. Place under broiler until meringue is browned. Serve immediately. Serves 6.

DIVINITY MERINGUE
3 extra-large egg whites
1 teaspoon white vinegar

$^1/_4$ cup white karo
$^1/_4$ cup confectioners' sugar

Beat egg whites until frothy, and add vinegar. Beat until meringue makes soft peaks. Add karo a little at a time, beating constantly. Repeat with confectioners' sugar, beating until meringue stands in peaks.

OLD–FASHIONED APPLE FRITTERS

Substitute bananas, peaches, or berries

1 cup sifted pastry flour
1 level teaspoon baking powder
1 level teaspoon confectioners' sugar
$^1/_4$ teaspoon salt

1 egg, slightly beaten
$^1/_4$ cup milk
2 apples, pared and cut into
  small pieces
Hot fat for frying

Sift together, three times, the flour, baking powder, sugar, and salt. Add the milk to the beaten egg and stir in the sifted ingredients. Then stir in the bits of apple. Drop the batter into the fat by spoonful and let fry until delicately browned. Drain on soft paper. Serve with confectioners' sugar, Jelly Sauce, or Vanilla Sauce. May also be served in a bowl with thick cream. Makes 12 to 15, depending on size.

Jelly Sauce: Melt jelly together with a small amount of water. Brandy, fruit brandy, or wine may be substituted for water.

VANILLA SAUCE

$^1/_2$ cup sugar
1 tablespoon cornstarch
1 cup boiling water

2 tablespoons butter
1 teaspoon vanilla extract
$^1/_8$ teaspoon salt

Mix sugar and cornstarch together in a saucepan. Stir in boiling water. Simmer for 5 minutes. Stir in butter and vanilla. Add salt. Serve warm. Makes $1^1/_4$ cups.

ARKANSAS FRUIT AND RICE FRITTERS

Pieces of fresh fruit are tucked into the fritters

¹/₄ cup rice, uncooked	1 level teaspoon baking powder
1 egg, slightly beaten	Slices of cooked peach or
¹/₂ cup milk	apple or uncooked berries
1¹/₂ cups sifted pastry flour	Hot fat for frying
¹/₂ teaspoon salt	Sugar

Cook the rice in boiling salted water until it is tender and
the water is absorbed or drained off; add the egg and milk;
then the flour, salt, and baking powder, sifted together
three times. Blend well. Take up by tablespoonsful, press
the fruit into the center of the mixture on the spoon, and
with a teaspoon scrape the whole into the hot fat. Fry to an
amber color. Serve with sprinkled sugar. Makes 12 to 15,
depending on size.

CHERRIES JUBILEE

Dazzle your guests with New Orleans glamour

$^1/_3$ cup sugar

2 tablespoons cornstarch

1 pound can dark, sweet, pitted
   cherries

$^1/_3$ cup brandy

Vanilla ice cream

Blend sugar and cornstarch in a saucepan. Drain cherries, reserving syrup. Slowly add syrup to dry ingredients, stirring well. Cook over medium heat, stirring constantly, until mixture is lightly thickened and smooth. Add cherries and remove from heat. Pour mixture into the top pan of a chafing dish, making certain the bottom pan is filled with hot water. Heat brandy until warm in a small pan. Ignite brandy with a long, wooden match, and pour over cherry mixture. Stir sauce until flame dies down. Place a scoop of vanilla ice cream in each of six bowls. Spoon sauce over ice cream and serve immediately. Serves 6.

Add a dash of almond extract to canned peach-pie and cherry-pie fillings.

FRUIT DESSERTS

BLACKBERRY ROLY–POLY WITH FRESH FRUIT SAUCE

A roly-poly is seen often in old Southern cookbooks

1 quart blackberries
$^1/_2$ cup water
$1^1/_4$ cups sugar
3 cups sifted flour
3 level teaspoons baking
   powder
$^1/_2$ teaspoon salt

$^1/_2$ cup shortening
1 egg yolk, beaten
Milk or water as needed
   (about 10 tablespoons)
1 egg white, slightly beaten
Sugar

In a heavy saucepan with high sides, cook berries with water for about 15 minutes or until soft and mushy. Press the mixture through a sieve to remove seeds. To the pulp add sugar and let simmer until well reduced. Keep half the mixture hot for a sauce and cool the rest. Sift together, three times, the flour, baking powder, and salt; work in the shortening, then mix to a dough with milk or water added to the beaten egg yolk. Knead slightly and roll into a sheet $^1/_4$ inch thick; cut into 8 or 10 rectangles; spread these with the cold blackberry mixture and roll over and over in a jelly roll fashion. Brush the top of each with the egg white, slightly beaten, and dredge with sugar. Bake at 350° for about 30 minutes or until lightly brown. Serve hot with the following blackberry sauce. If desired, top with a small amount of whipped cream sweetened with confectioners' sugar.

BLACKBERRY SAUCE

Remaining blackberry mixture $^1/_4$ cup blackberry wine (or
                                          to taste)

Mix together and reheat to serve. Serves 8 to 10.

BLACKBERRY MOUSSE

An heirloom dessert from Mobile

1¹/₂ tablespoons gelatin
¹/₄ cup cold water
1 cup fresh orange juice
1 tablespoon cornstarch
Grated rind of 1 orange
1¹/₂ pints fresh blackberries, washed and dried, or 3 16-ounce waterpack cans, drained

4 egg yolks
1 cup sugar
¹/₂ teaspoon cinnamon
1¹/₂ cups heavy cream
¹/₂ cup confectioners' sugar
4 egg whites
Pinch salt
1 tablespoon sugar
Berries for garnish

In a small glass bowl soften gelatin in cold water 5 to 6 minutes. In a saucepan place 1 cup fresh orange juice, cornstarch, orange peel, and ³/₄ cup berries. Add softened gelatin and heat carefully, stirring until slightly thickened, about 10 minutes. Remove from heat and cool to room temperature. Beat egg yolks, adding 1 cup sugar gradually; add cinnamon. Place in top of a double boiler until mixture is too hot to touch. Stir yolk mixture into gelatin mixture and cool to room temperature. Whip cream and fold into cooled berry mixture. In a blender, purée remaining berries with ¹/₂ cup confectioners' sugar. Stir into the mixture with a knife until it streaks with a marbled effect. Beat egg whites with a pinch of salt and 1 tablespoon sugar until stiff but not dry. Fold into berry mixture and chill in a 2-quart soufflé dish or greased ring mold. Garnish with berries. Serves 8.

EOLA HOTEL'S HOT PEAR AND RASPBERRY COMPOTE

Natchez's oldest hotel, restored recently to its former grace and beauty

2 quarts pears, poached, sliced
1 quart raspberries, fresh or frozen
1 quart mandarin orange sections, drained
1 quart apricot halves, drained
1 cup port wine
4 cups fresh grated coconut or flaked, sweetened coconut
2 cups brown sugar
1 cup heavy cream, whipped

Poach pears by dropping halves into boiling water to cover. Reduce heat at once and simmer until barely tender. Remove them from the heat and drain immediately afterwards, so that they will not continue to cook and get mushy. Slice the pears and mix with raspberries, mandarin orange sections, drained apricot halves, and port wine. Place in an oblong shallow casserole. Mix brown sugar and coconut together. Scatter it over the fruit and port wine mixture. Bake in a preheated 400° oven 15 to 20 minutes or until lightly brown and fruit is hot. Serve warm in footed goblets. Top with whipped cream. Serves 8 if using $^3/_4$-cup servings.

STRAWBERRY SHORTCAKE

Closing stanza of many a Sunday dinner

2 cups flour
3 teaspoons baking powder
$^1/_2$ teaspoon salt
2 tablespoons sugar
$^1/_8$ teaspoon nutmeg
$^1/_2$ cup unsalted butter
$^3/_4$ cup milk

1 tablespoon melted butter
1 tablespoon sugar
1 quart strawberries
$^1/_2$ cup sugar
$^1/_2$ pint whipping cream
4 tablespoons sugar
1 teaspoon vanilla

Mix dry ingredients. Cut in butter in a food processor until mixture is the texture of coarse meal. Add milk. Toss on floured board and roll dough until 1 inch thick. Cut into rounds with a biscuit cutter. Brush with melted butter. Sprinkle with 1 tablespoon sugar. Bake at 400° for 15 minutes or until light golden. Slice strawberries and stir in $^1/_2$ cup sugar. Let sit at room temperature for 1 hour or until juicy. May refrigerate until serving time. Whip cream and season with 4 tablespoons sugar and vanilla. Split biscuits, fill with berries, and top with whipped cream. Serves 8 to 10.

BAKED STUFFED PEACHES WITH CUSTARD SAUCE

A real Southern treat

8 medium-sized ripe peaches
1 tablespoon lemon juice
$^1/_2$ cup finely chopped candied ginger
$^1/_2$ cup finely chopped pecans

$^1/_2$ cup honey, divided
$^1/_4$ cup cookie or cake crumbs
Custard sauce or whipped
   cream, sweetened

Dip peaches in boiling water for the count of 10. Remove and peel. Drop in water to cover with lemon juice. Leave until all are prepared. Mix chopped ginger, pecans, honey, and cookie crumbs. Cut peaches in half and remove stones. Place about 2 tablespoons of the nut mixture in each peach and put back together, fastening well with toothpicks. Place peaches in a baking pan just large enough to hold them and pour remaining honey over. Cover and bake at 350° until peaches are tender, about 30 minutes. Serve warm with custard sauce. Serves 8.

CUSTARD SAUCE

1$^1/_2$ tablespoons cornstarch
2 cups light cream, divided
4 egg yolks

$^1/_2$ cup sugar
1 teaspoon vanilla

Dissolve cornstarch in $^1/_4$ cup cream. Beat egg yolks until light, then combine with cornstarch mixture. Heat remaining cream, taking care not to boil, and add sugar. Pour 1 cup hot cream and sugar over egg mixture, stirring constantly. Return remaining hot cream to low heat, stir in egg-cream mixture, and continue to stir and cook 5 minutes until sauce is slightly thickened. Add vanilla, blend thoroughly, and cool.

BANANAS FOSTER

Spectacular showstopper that's easy to make

2 tablespoons butter	$^1/_4$ teaspoon cinnamon
4 tablespoons brown sugar	1 ounce banana liqueur
2 bananas, peeled, halved, and sliced lengthwise	2 ounces rum
	Vanilla ice cream

Melt butter in a large skillet or chafing dish. Stir in brown sugar, slowly, and cook until bubbly. Add bananas and sauté on both sides until barely tender, basting constantly. Sprinkle bananas with cinnamon. Heat banana liqueur and rum in a small boiler. Pour over fruit and flame with a long, wooden match. Baste bananas with liquid until flames die. Scoop vanilla ice cream into two dessert dishes, spoon banana mixture over ice cream and serve at once. Serves 2.

Bananas Foster was created by Brennan's Restaurant in New Orleans and is on the menu at the popular "Breakfast at Brennan's." The dessert was named for Richard Foster, a patron of the restaurant.

Strawberries marinated in port wine for a few hours are wonderful.

ICE CREAM AND DESSERT BEVERAGES

Ice cream is one of the South's special delights. Simmering July days and sultry August nights create a craving for the coldest food available—often a bowlful of the frosty delicacy. Not only does ice cream cool our bodies, it fills our souls with nostalgia. Many of us remember childhood afternoons spent dancing around the groaning freezer, waiting for that labored halt which meant the dasher was ready to be licked. Southerners are also fond of refreshing dessert beverages, often made with ice cream, which are served at parties throughout the year.

One of the South's earliest ice cream devotees was George Washington, who had a "cream machine for making ice" installed at Mount Vernon. During the summer of 1790, Washington spent approximately two hundred dollars on the refreshing dessert, but unfortunately, Martha neglected to leave her recipe behind.

Thomas Jefferson was the first president to bequeath a recipe to posterity—one he acquired in France while serving as ambassador and recorded in his own hand. Using the French method of initially making a custard with egg yolks, he prepared the dessert in a machine called a "sorbetière." Later, during Jefferson's presidency, a White House visitor reported that ice cream balls enclosed in warm pastry shells were presented—an ambitious dish for the time.

Dolley Madison served ice cream frequently during the 1800s when her husband, James, was president. At this time, restaurants such as New Orleans Exchange Coffee House listed it on the menu.

During the late nineteenth century, Northern businessmen made freezing ice cream easier when they began packing large blocks of winter ice in sawdust and shipping it to the sizzling South. Soon, horse-drawn ice wagons were a welcome sight on Southern streets.

Today, freezing ice cream is as traditional during a Southern summer as grilling hamburgers and chilling watermelon.

FAYE COLEMAN'S CHOCOLATE ICE CREAM

Smooth, creamy, melt-in-your-mouth chocolate

1¹/₂ cups sugar
2 tablespoons flour
¹/₈ teaspoon salt
4 tablespoons cocoa
2¹/₂ cups milk
5 eggs, beaten

1 can sweetened condensed
   milk
1 pint light cream
1 pint heavy cream
2 tablespoons vanilla

In a heavy boiler, combine sugar, flour, salt, and cocoa. Stir until combined thoroughly. Add 2¹/₂ cups milk, beaten eggs, condensed milk, light, and heavy creams to the above mixture. Cook on medium heat until mixture barely coats tip of spoon. Remove from burner and add vanilla. Let mixture cool. When cooled, fill freezer with mixture—if needed, finish filling freezer with whole milk (this usually is necessary). Makes 1 gallon.

MISSISSIPPI BLUEBERRY ICE CREAM

A luscious taste treat

4 cups fresh blueberries	2 tablespoons cherry-flavored
3^1/$_2$ cups sugar, divided	brandy
3 tablespoons lemon juice	1 tablespoon vanilla extract
4 eggs	4 cups whipping cream

Combine blueberries, 1 cup sugar, and lemon juice in the container of an electric blender; process until puréed. Set aside. Beat eggs until thick and lemon-colored. Gradually add remaining 2 ^{1}/$_2$ cups sugar, beating constantly. Add brandy, vanilla, and puréed blueberries; continue beating until well-blended. Pour mixture into freezer can of a 1-gallon hand-turned or electric freezer. Add whipping cream and freeze according to manufacturer's directions. Let ripen 2 hours before serving. Makes about 1 gallon.

This special recipe was developed by Ann Rushing, Marketing Specialist for the Mississippi Department of Agriculture and Commerce. Ann is also a columnist for the Clarion Ledger *and* Jackson Daily News. *Her "Let's Go to Market" column and television shows have been enjoyed by Mississippians for many years.*

PRALINES 'N CREAM ICE CREAM

Praline chunks in creamy, uncooked custard

8 eggs

2 cups sugar

1 can (12 ounces) evaporated milk

3 pints light cream

1 1/2 teaspoons vanilla

1/8 teaspoon salt

8 pralines, crumbled

Beat eggs well and gradually add sugar. Slowly mix in evaporated milk, light cream, vanilla, and salt. Stir in crumbled pralines and freeze in ice cream maker. Makes 1 gallon.

DOT'S FRESH PEACH ICE CREAM

Celebrate summer with this sensational cooler

6 eggs
3/4 cup sugar
1 can condensed milk
2 cartons heavy cream
1 pint light cream

2 cups milk
Pinch of salt
4 teaspoons vanilla
3 cups mashed ripe peaches
(sweetened with 1 cup
sugar)

Beat eggs; gradually add sugar. Mix in remaining ingredients (except peaches). For best results, mash peaches in a food processor. Pour mixture into ice cream freezer container and add peaches just before ice cream begins to harden. Finish freezing. Makes 1 gallon.

MARY COOKE'S CARAMEL TOFFEE CREATION

Vanilla ice cream and Caramel Toffee Sauce—an unforgettable combination

$^1/_3$ cup brown sugar
$1^1/_2$ cups flour
1 cup pecans, chopped
1 cup butter or margarine,
  melted

$1^1/_2$ cups Caramel Toffee Sauce
$^1/_2$ gallon vanilla ice cream,
  softened

Stir together brown sugar, flour, pecans, and melted butter or margarine. Spread mixture thinly on a greased cookie sheet and bake at 350° for approximately 20 minutes or until done. Be careful that it does not burn. Cool and crumble half of crumbs onto bottom of a glass 13 x 9 inch baking dish. Spread half of Caramel Toffee Sauce over crumbs. Fill dish with spoonsful of vanilla ice cream. Add rest of Caramel Toffee Sauce and top with remaining crumbs. Freeze. Serves 12 to 16.

CARAMEL TOFFEE SAUCE
Sinfully delicious!

2 cups light brown sugar,
   packed
2 cups dark brown sugar,
   packed

4 tablespoons butter
1 pint heavy cream
1 tablespoon vanilla

Combine the sugars, butter, and cream. Cook in the top of a double boiler over medium heat until it will coat the back of a spoon. Add vanilla. Cover and store in the refrigerator. Makes $2^1/_2$ cups.

SOUTHERN FRUIT SHERBET
Delicious with almost any fruit in season

$^1/_4$ cup fresh orange juice
$^1/_2$ cup fresh lemon juice
$1^1/_2$ cups sugar
1 quart milk
1 cup of any of the following
   fruits: crushed strawberries,
crushed raspberries, apricot
pulp, mashed peaches,
mashed bananas, finely
chopped pears, apple sauce,
blueberries

Mix the orange juice, lemon juice, and sugar. Add milk slowly while stirring. (If mixture curdles it will freeze smooth again.) Add chosen fruit. Pour into a freezer container, following the manufacturer's directions for freezing. Makes about 2 quarts.

TRILBY'S CREME DE MENTHE MERINGUE DESSERT

A Gulf Coast tradition, the restaurant is located in Ocean Springs, Mississippi

4 large egg whites	$^1/_4$ cup pecans, chopped
$^1/_4$ teaspoon cream of tartar	French vanilla ice cream
2 ounces green crème de menthe	Whipped cream
	Chopped pecans, shaved
1 cup sugar	chocolate (optional)

Place egg whites in a warm mixing bowl. Add cream of tartar and liqueur to egg whites. Whip mixture until fluffy. Add sugar, one teaspoon at a time, and continue to whip until very stiff, but not dried out. Gently fold in chopped pecans. Line a baking sheet with parchment or brown paper. Drop large spoonsful of meringue mixture onto the baking sheet and form nests with the back of the spoon. Bake at 225° for 1 hour and 15 minutes; turn the oven off, leaving meringues to dry in oven (this can take from 1 to 4 hours, depending on humidity level). Carefully peel paper off the shells. Makes 8 to 10 shells.

To garnish: Each meringue shell is filled with a generous scoop of French vanilla ice cream, topped with Trilby's Chocolate Sauce, whipped cream, and a sprinkle of finely chopped pecans and chocolate shavings.

TRILBY'S CHOCOLATE SAUCE

$^1/_2$ pound butter	1 12-ounce can evaporated milk
$^3/_4$ cup cocoa	$1^1/_2$ teaspoons vanilla
3 cups sugar	

Melt butter in top of a double boiler. Add cocoa and blend well. Add sugar gradually, blend well, and cook for 15 minutes. Add milk and cook for 15 minutes longer. Remove from double boiler and cool. Add vanilla. Makes about 1 quart.

HEAVENLY SURPRISE DESSERT

Coffee ice cream and Bourbon Caramel Sauce buried under a cloud of whipped cream

1 quart coffee ice cream
8 amaretto (almond flavored) cookies
1 recipe Bourbon Caramel Sauce (see below)

1 pint heavy cream, whipped
Maraschino cherries for garnish

For each serving, place an amaretto cookie or almond-flavored sugar cookie in the bottom of a sherbet dish. Place a scoop of coffee ice cream over it and spoon the Bourbon Caramel Sauce over all. Cover with whipped cream and garnish with a cherry. Serves 8.

BOURBON CARAMEL SAUCE

1 cup light cream
$^1/_2$ cup butter
1 cup brown sugar, packed

$^1/_3$ cup chopped nuts, toasted
$^1/_4$ cup bourbon

Warm the cream and cream together the butter and sugar. Gradually stir the warmed cream into the butter and sugar mixture. Stir over low heat until the mixture boils. Remove from the heat and stir in the nuts and bourbon. This is also delicious over baked custard or bread pudding. The sauce may be kept in the refrigerator for several days and reheated slightly before serving. Makes about $2^1/_2$ cups.

COTILLION PUNCH
Zesty thirst-quencher for festive occasions

$^1/_2$ gallon pineapple sherbet
2 (32-ounce) bottles cranberry
   juice, chilled.

2 (32-ounce) bottles ginger
   ale, chilled.

Soften sherbet and mash until slightly mushy. Place in punch bowl. Pour in chilled juice and ginger ale. Serves 5

HOPE FARM EGGNOG

Heirloom recipe from a Natchez mansion

18 egg yolks   2 quarts heavy cream
2 cups sugar   18 egg whites, beaten well
1 fifth bourbon whiskey   Nutmeg

Beat egg yolks. Add sugar gradually, beating well. Slowly add whiskey and unbeaten heavy cream. Gently fold in egg whites. Serve in a punch bowl; sprinkle nutmeg on top. Serves 20. For the calorie conscious: Substitute 2 quarts light cream for the heavy cream. Use only 9 egg whites.

This recipe belonged to the late Mrs. J. Balfour Miller, who founded the Natchez Pilgrimage. Every Christmas morning, Mr. and Mrs. Miller, who had no children, invited their friends with their children and grandchildren for eggnog at Hope Farm, their antebellum home.

COLONIAL SYLLABUB
An old Southern holiday beverage or dessert

1 pint heavy cream, whipped
³/₄ cup confectioners' sugar
¹/₂ cup white wine
4 tablespoons sherry wine

1 teaspoon lemon juice
Few grains of salt
Nutmeg

Whip cream until stiff, gradually adding sugar. Mix in wines and seasonings. Serve at once in cups; sprinkle with nutmeg. This dessert does not hold well. Serves 8.

Syllabub was a popular dessert beverage in the colonial South, particularly in Virginia and Maryland. The easiest method for preparing the foaming concoction was to take a bowl of wine to the barn and draw milk from the cow straight into the bowl, making a bubbly punch.

PIES AND COBBLERS

When the first English settlers sailed for Virginia, they packed their pie recipes along with their luggage. Southerners have cherished the tradition ever since. Originally they followed the British rule of using two crusts, but soon eliminated the upper crust in favor of open pastry shells called "coffins." A cornucopia of ingredients awaited their pie-making skills: pumpkins, sweet potatoes, berries, and pecans. They quickly learned to dry fruit and store nuts in order to enjoy pies during the cold winters.

When fruit and nuts were unavailable, they turned to custards, especially chess pie which is still revered as a true Southern classic. The rich, sugary dessert inspired innumerable variations, depending on what the cook had in the pantry—Lemon Chess, Chocolate Chess, Japanese Fruit, and Jeff Davis, seasoned with cinnamon and nutmeg.

By 1830, pie making was so widely practiced in the South that a special piece of furniture called a "pie safe" became a fixture in many kitchens. A wooden cabinet with tin doors decorated with perforated holes, the pie safe protected its contents from insects, the hot sun, and greedy fingers.

Over the years, additions were made to the repertoire of Southern pie bakers. Meringue as a topping came into being in the late nineteenth century and is used today, especially on lemon, coconut, and chocolate cream pies. Another nineteenth century innovation was the use of crumb crusts: graham cracker, vanilla wafer, and chocolate cookie.

Modern refrigeration was the biggest boon to pie making. How easy to thicken your pie in the refrigerator, confident that the filling will hold and any mistakes will be camouflaged by a cloud of whipped cream. Although methods may be modernized, the tradition of baking pies will always be an integral part of Southern cuisine.

KEY LIME PIE

It's easy to make this tasty, tangy treat

4 eggs, separated
1 14-ounce can sweetened
    condensed milk
$^1/_2$ cup lime juice

1 prepared graham cracker
    crust
$^1/_4$ teaspoon cream of tartar
4 tablespoons sugar

Beat egg yolks until light, mix in condensed milk, and slowly add lime juice. Beat mixture briefly until thick and pour into graham cracker crust. Beat egg whites; add cream of tartar; gradually beat in sugar. When mixture holds stiff peaks, smooth it over pie. Bake at 350° for approximately 15 minutes until meringue is golden brown. Chill at least 3 hours before serving. Serves 6 to 8.

Key Lime Pie became popular in the Florida Keys when sweetened condensed milk was introduced in 1856. Cows were scarce in the area, so residents were delighted with the milk and combined it with the tart limes to create a pie. True key limes are grown only in the Keys, so Persian limes, available at most food stores, may be used in this recipe.

PIES AND COBBLERS

GEORGIANNE'S PEACHES 'N CREAM PIE

Summertime is peach time in the Deep South

1 cup sour cream
$^2/_3$ cup sugar
2 tablespoons flour
$^1/_8$ teaspoon salt
$^1/_2$ teaspoon cinnamon

1 teaspoon vanilla
1 egg
$2^1/_3$ cups peaches, diced
1 8-inch pie shell, unbaked

Cream the sour cream and sugar and beat in the flour, salt, cinnamon, vanilla, and egg. Stir peaches into mixture; pour into unbaked pie shell; bake at 375° for 35 minutes.

TOPPING

$^1/_3$ cup brown sugar
$^1/_4$ cup flour

$^1/_4$ teaspoon cinnamon
$^1/_4$ cup butter, cut into slivers

Mix ingredients together. Sprinkle over pie and bake 25 more minutes or until firm. Serves 6.

MOTHER'S PEAR MINCE– MEAT PIE

A Christmas tradition at Jo's house

3 cups prepared mincemeat
1 egg
$^1/_3$ cup milk
1 tablespoon flour
1 tart apple, peeled and finely
  diced

$^1/_2$ cup pecans or walnuts,
chopped
2 to 3 tablespoons brandy
Pastry for double-crusted 9-
  inch pie

Place mincemeat in a bowl. Beat egg slightly and add milk and flour. Mix with the apple and nuts. Add to the mincemeat mixture. Add the brandy, mixing well. Pour into an unbaked 9-inch pie shell. Cover with a top crust or a lattice crust and bake at 450° in a preheated oven for 10 minutes. Reduce heat to 350° and bake for 30 more minutes. Serves 8.

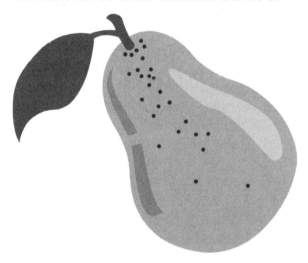

PIES AND COBBLERS

DEEP SOUTH SWEET POTATO PIE

Serve plain or the old-fashioned way—spread with a tart jelly and covered with meringue

1 1/2 cups sweet potatoes, boiled and mashed (canned may be used)
4 eggs
1/3 cup sugar
2 tablespoons honey
3/4 teaspoon cinnamon
1/4 teaspoon nutmeg
1/8 teaspoon ground ginger
1 cup light cream
1/8 teaspoon salt
1 teaspoon vanilla flavoring
1 9-inch pie shell, unbaked

Mash the boiled sweet potatoes with a mixer until smooth. Beat 4 eggs very lightly and add to the sweet potatoes. Stir in the sugar and beat all together. Add honey, cinnamon, and nutmeg with the ground ginger, cream, salt, and vanilla flavoring, mixing to blend. Pour the mixture into an unbaked pie shell and bake in a preheated 450° oven for 10 minutes. Reduce the temperature to 350° and bake for 30 minutes longer, or until a knife inserted near the pie's center comes out clean. At this point the pie may be cooled and served with dollops of whipped cream or plain with a cold glass of sweet milk. Pie may also be served spread with 1/2 cup melted tart jelly over the baked pie, then spread with a meringue and browned. Serves 6 to 8.

This is the sweet potato pie recipe that was selected to represent the best in Mississippi cuisine at the 1967 Mississippi Marketing Council at Anuga, Cologne, Germany, and the United States Trade Center in London, England. It was kitchen tested by Bobby Ginn, who was then chef at the old Heidelberg Hotel in Jackson.

LOUREA'S SWEET POTATO PIE

Similar to a chess pie, sweet and utterly delicious

1 cup sweet potatoes, mashed
5 eggs
3 cups sugar
4 tablespoons flour
³/₄ cup butter or margarine,
  melted

1 14-ounce can sweetened
  condensed milk
¹/₂ teaspoon vanilla flavor
¹/₂ teaspoon nutmeg
19-inch pie shell, unbaked

You may use canned sweet potatoes, drained to equal 1 cup, but pared and cooked sweet potatoes freshly dug are traditional. Boil 2 or 3 sweet potatoes in salted water until tender. Peel and mash with slightly beaten eggs, sugar, flour, melted butter, condensed milk, vanilla, and nutmeg. Pour into prepared pie crust and bake at 400° for 15 minutes, then reduce heat to 300° and cook 1 hour or until a knife inserted in the center comes out clean. Pie freezes well. Serves 8.

GREAT PUMPKIN PIE
Best when a whole pumpkin is used

1 whole pumpkin or 1 18-
   ounce can to equal 1$^3/_4$ cups
$^3/_4$ cup raisins, preferably white
$^1/_2$ teaspoon salt
1$^3/_4$ cups half-and-half cream
3 eggs
$^2/_3$ cup dark brown sugar,
   packed

2 tablespoons molasses
2 teaspoons cinnamon
$^1/_4$ teaspoon cloves
$^1/_2$ teaspoon ginger
$^1/_2$ teaspoon nutmeg
$^3/_4$ cup chopped toasted
   pecans
1 9-inch pie shell, unbaked

If using whole pumpkin, scoop out the inside. (Save seeds for toasting another time.) Cut pumpkin into large chunks, peel off outer skin, and dice. Place in unseasoned water and cook until very tender. Mash with an electric mixer or food processor. In a saucepan, with enough water to cover them, boil raisins for 2 minutes. Drain and set aside. Blend the remaining ingredients, except pecans. Add raisins and stir in pecans. Fill uncooked pie shell and bake at 425° for 45 to 50 minutes or until a knife comes out clean. Both the filling and cooked pumpkin will freeze. Pumpkin pie may be served plain, with dollops of whipped cream, or is delicious with a ginger sauce. Serves 6 to 8.

The first pumpkin pie wasn't a pie at all: it was a whole pumpkin with the top sliced out, filled with milk, spices, and honey and baked in hot ashes! The North American Indians sliced pumpkins into long slices and roasted them over the open fire. It wasn't long before Early American housewives learned to split open the pumpkins, remove the seeds, put the halves back together and roast the whole pumpkins in the hearth ovens. Soon the Southern colonists were creating our favorites of today with the pumpkin pulp.

MY GRANDMOTHER'S DEEP-DISH APPLE PIE

Apples, cinnamon, and brown sugar—perfect for fall

5-6 cups apples, pared and
    cut into small pieces
$^3/_4$ cup light brown sugar
2 tablespoons flour

$^1/_4$ teaspoon cinnamon
1 tablespoon lemon juice
1 tablespoon or more butter
1 pie crust, unbaked

Toss apple pieces, brown sugar, flour, cinnamon, and lemon juice in a bowl until apple pieces are well coated. Place them in a deep pie plate or casserole. Dot with butter. Top with a pie crust, bringing edges over sides of dish and pressing them with a fork. Prick crust in several places with fork. Bake at 350° for 30-40 minutes or until done. Serve plain or with cream or hard sauce. Serves 6 to 8.

PIES AND COBBLERS

MOM'S APPLE PIE

Jo's children's favorite pie

3 cups tart apples	¹/₄ teaspoon nutmeg
¹/₄ cup sugar	2 tablespoons butter, melted
2 tablespoons flour	¹/₂ cup brown sugar, packed
1 tablespoon lemon juice	Pastry for double-crusted 9-
¹/₄ teaspoon cinnamon	inch pie

Peel and slice the apples thinly. Combine the sugar, flour, lemon juice, cinnamon, nutmeg, melted butter, and brown sugar. Stir into the apples, coating them well. Pour into unbaked pie shell. Top with remaining pastry. Cut slits in the top of the pastry and brush with a beaten egg mixed with a teaspoon of water. Bake in a pre-heated 400° oven for 45 minutes. Serves 6.

When placing dough into a pie pan, roll it onto your rolling pin. Unroll it onto the pan.

AUNT CARO'S CHOCOLATE PIE

A sought-after "secret recipe"

3 cups sugar
³/₄ cup flour
5 tablespoons cocoa
8 egg yolks, slightly beaten
1 12-ounce can evaporated
   milk
1 cup water

3 tablespoons butter
2 teaspoons vanilla
2 9-inch pie shells, baked and
   cooled
8 egg whites
¹/₃ teaspoon salt
1 cup sugar

Mix the dry ingredients. Add slightly beaten egg yolks to milk and water; add to dry ingredients. Cook slowly over low heat, stirring constantly until thickened. Add butter and vanilla; mix well. Pour into cooled pie shells. Make meringue by beating egg whites until foamy; add salt. Add sugar one tablespoon at a time while beating. Beat until stiff peaks form, but not dry. Spread on filled pie shells, sealing edges carefully. Bake in a preheated 325° oven for 15 minutes or until lightly browned. Serves 6 to 8.

Aunt Caro was Post Mistress in a small town in Mississippi for forty years. Every special occasion called for one of her chocolate meringue pies. When people begged for the recipe she would just smile and bake them a pie—still not revealing the recipe. Virginia Carlton asked for the recipe when she was a young bride marrying into the Carlton family. Aunt Caro gave it to her but made her promise not to reveal the secret until her death.

COCONUT CREAM PIE
Serve anytime—it is always welcome

1³/₄ cups milk
³/₄ cup sugar
¹/₂ teaspoon salt
3¹/₂ tablespoons flour
2 tablespoons cornstarch
1 egg plus 3 egg yolks, beaten
2 tablespoons butter
¹/₂ teaspoon vanilla

¹/₄ teaspoon almond extract
1 cup grated coconut (if
   using fresh grated coconut
   save 1 tablespoon of the
   milk)
¹/₂ cup heavy cream
1 9-inch pie crust, baked
3 egg whites

Scald half of the milk and add ¹/₂ cup of the sugar and the salt. Bring to a boil. Mix flour, cornstarch, and beaten egg and yolks with the remaining milk. Beat until smooth. Add a little of the hot milk and blend. Combine both mixtures and cook over hot water in a double boiler until thick, stirring constantly. Remove from heat. Add butter and flavoring. Beat with a wooden spoon until smooth. Add ³/₄ cup of coconut (and the tablespoon of milk if you used fresh coconut). Whip the heavy cream and fold it into the mixture. Pour mixture into the baked pie crust. Beat the egg whites until frothy. Add remaining sugar and beat until stiff. Smooth the meringue over the pie and sprinkle with the remaining ¹/₄ cup of coconut. Place in a 450° oven until the coconut begins to brown. Serves 6 to 8.

CHOCOLATE FUDGE PIE

Marvelous alone, superb topped with vanilla ice cream

1 stick butter	1 cup sugar
3 squares unsweetened chocolate	Dash of salt
	1 teaspoon vanilla
4 eggs	1 19-inch pie shell, unbaked
3 tablespoons white karo	

Melt butter and chocolate in top of a double boiler. Cool slightly. Beat eggs with mixer until thick. Mix in syrup, sugar, salt, and vanilla. Add chocolate mixture. Combine well and pour into pie shell. Bake at 350° for 25 to 30 minutes, or until filling is set but slightly soft. It will become firmer when cool. Serves 6 to 8.

CROSS CREEK'S BLACK BOTTOM PIE

The Yearling was written at Cross Creek, located in the Florida Everglades

14 crisp ginger cookies, crumbled fine	5 tablespoons butter, melted

Mix the crumbs and butter together and line a pie plate with the mixture. Bake at 250° for 10 minutes. Cool.

BASIC FILLING

1 tablespoon gelatin	1 tablespoon cornstarch
4 tablespoons cold water	$^1/_8$ teaspoon salt
$1^3/_4$ cups milk	4 egg yolks, beaten
$^1/_2$ cup sugar	

CHOCOLATE LAYER

2 squares chocolate, melted	1 teaspoon vanilla

RUM LAYER

4 egg whites	$^1/_2$ cup sugar
$^1/_8$ teaspoon cream of tartar	1 tablespoon rum

TOPPING

1 cup heavy cream	Chocolate, grated
2 tablespoons confectioners' sugar	

Soak gelatin in cold water. Scald milk and add sugar mixed with cornstarch, salt, and beaten yolks. Cook in a double boiler, stirring constantly until it coats the back of a spoon. Stir in dissolved gelatin. Divide custard in half. To one half, add melted chocolate and vanilla. Turn while hot into cooled crust, dipping carefully so as not to ruin crust. Cool remaining half of custard. Beat whites and cream of tartar, adding sugar slowly. Blend with cooled custard; add rum. Spread carefully over chocolate layer. Chill thoroughly, even overnight. When ready to serve, whip cream with the confectioners' sugar. Pile on top of pie; sprinkle with grated chocolate. Serves 6-8.

Mary Leigh's brother, Roy Hendee, found this recipe in Highland School Parent Teacher Association Cook Book, *published in 1950. It was submitted by Mrs. B. G. Rawlins. A chocolate wafer crust may be substituted, if desired.*

For baking unfilled pie shells, prick all over with tines of fork or weight the bottom of crust with dried beans or rice. Remove the beans or rice a few minutes before baking time is over.

BETTY EVERETT'S PECAN PIE

A Southern classic that is surprisingly easy to make

$^1/_2$ stick margarine, softened
$^1/_2$ cup sugar
4 large eggs, slightly beaten
1 cup light corn syrup
$^1/_2$ teaspoon vanilla

$^1/_8$ teaspoon salt
1 cup chopped pecans
1 9-inch pie shell, unbaked
$^1/_4$ cup pecan halves

Cream margarine and sugar well. Add beaten eggs and blend well. Add light corn syrup, vanilla, and salt. Stir in chopped pecans and pour mixture into unbaked pie shell. Arrange pecan halves on top for decoration. Bake at 350° for 1 hour. Serves 8.

PIES AND COBBLERS

WESTBROOK'S GRASSHOPPER PIE
Wonderful anytime, but especially after a seafood dinner

1 (8$^1/_2$ -ounce) box chocolate
wafers, crushed fine

$^3/_4$ stick butter, melted

Mix crumbs and butter (reserving $^1/_4$ cup crumbs for topping). Press crumb mixture into a 9-inch pan and chill.

FILLING

6 tablespoons crème de menthe
3 tablespoons clear crème de
cacao
36 large marshmallows

2 heaping tablespoons vanilla
ice cream
1$^1/_2$ cartons heavy cream

Heat crème de menthe, crème de cacao, and marshmallows in top of double boiler until marshmallows are melted. Cool. Add ice cream to heavy cream and whip until very stiff. Gently fold in cooled marshmallow mixture until blended well. Pour into chilled pie crust and sprinkle reserved crumbs over top. Refrigerate. Better if made the day before serving. Serves 6 to 8.

GRANDMOTHER'S PEACH COBBLER

Melts in your mouth

1 cup flour	1^1/$_2$ cups sugar
^{1}/$_8$ teaspoon salt	2 tablespoons flour
^{1}/$_2$ cup shortening	^{1}/$_8$ teaspoon cinnamon
3 tablespoons ice water	^{1}/$_8$ teaspoon almond extract
^{1}/$_2$ cup butter	Beaten egg white
4 cups peaches (about 9	Sugar
medium), peeled and sliced	Cream
1^1/$_2$ cups water	

Combine first 3 ingredients with a fork or pastry blender to make pastry. Add ice water. Form dough. Wrap in wax paper and chill for 8 hours. When ready to make the cobbler, roll out pastry and cut into strips. Reserve enough strips to make a lattice top on cobbler. Place remaining strips on a cookie sheet and bake at 450° for 10 minutes or until crisp. To make the filling, mix butter, peaches, and water in a saucepan. Bring to a boil. Blend sugar, flour, and cinnamon, stirring into boiling mixture until dissolved. Remove from heat and add almond extract. Grease an 8 ^{1}/$_2$ x 9 ^{1}/$_2$ inch baking dish. Place half the peach mixture in dish; top with cooked pastry strips. Add remaining peach mixture and place uncooked pastry strips over top in lattice fashion. Brush with beaten egg white and sprinkle with a little sugar. Bake at 375° for 35 to 40 minutes. Serve warm with cream. Serves 8.

DEEP-DISH BLACKBERRY COBBLER
Juicy and crusty

1 cup flour	1 cup sugar
$1/8$ teaspoon salt	2 tablespoons cornstarch
$1/2$ cup shortening	6 tablespoons butter
3 tablespoons ice water	Beaten egg white
6 cups blackberries, divided	Sugar

Combine first 3 ingredients with a fork or a pastry blender to make pastry. Add ice water. Form dough. Wrap in wax paper and chill for 8 hours. When ready to make the cobbler, roll out pastry and cut half of the dough into strips. Reserve the other half of dough for the top crust. Place remaining strips on a cookie sheet and bake at 450° for 10 minutes or until crisp. Cover 4 cups blackberries with water, barely covering. Cook over medium heat until berries are tender. Mash berries through sieve. Add sugar, cornstarch, butter, and remaining 2 cups blackberries. Bring to a boil. Stir and remove from heat. Grease an $8^1/_2$ x $9^1/_2$ inch baking dish. Place half of the blackberry mixture in dish; top with cooked pastry strips. Add remaining blackberry mixture and place uncooked pastry over the top. Brush with beaten egg white and sprinkle with a little sugar. Bake at 375° for 35 minutes or until brown. Serve warm as is or splash with blackberry brandy and top with whipped cream sweetened with confectioners' sugar. Serves 8.

PIES AND COBBLERS

INDEX

INDEX